Reaching New Heights Through Kindness In Marriage

Miriam Yerushalmi

Illustrated by

Rae Shagalov

Text Copyright 2021 Miriam Yerushalyim
Illustrations Copyright 2021 Rae Shagalov

All Rights Reserved.
No part of this book may be reproduced or transmitted by any form or by any means, electronic or mechanical, without prior written consent from the author.

Printed in the United States of America
First Printing 2021
ISBN: 978-1-7347581-4-6

This workbook is based on and designed to complement Miriam Yerushalmi's books: *Reaching New Heights Through Kindness in Marriage* (original edition) and *Reaching New Heights Through Kindness in Marriage: Universal Edition*.

Miriam's books, which currently include four titles in the *Reaching New Heights* self-help series and 15 children's books, are available at reachingnewheights.co and on Amazon.

Please do not color on Shabbat or Jewish holy days, as writing and coloring are prohibited by Jewish Law on those days.

TESTIMONIALS

In this workbook, Miriam Yerushalmi presents exercises and meditations that will help you easily integrate her teachings to strengthen your marriage. Whatever stage you are at in your marriage—whether you are newlywed and want to start out strong, or have been married for years and want to change the direction of your marital relationship—these techniques will imbue you with positivity and have a beneficial impact on all your relationships.

The accompanying artwork can be enjoyed on its own, or utilized as an extra fun, therapeutic activity. Relax and release your inner artist, as you create masterpieces on the page — and in your marriage.

"Miriam Yerushalmi is an astounding therapist who is devoted to helping women in need and is successful in treating them. I believe her Reaching New Heights series has a lot of knowledge to offer and will be an inspiring read to all."
—Rabbi Dr. Abraham J. Twerski, Founder and Medical Director Emeritus, Gateway Rehabilitation Center

"Miriam Yerushalmi has taught her holistic CBTT™ brain training techniques at our Evolutions Treatment Center with amazing success. The beneficial effects of applying her advice, exercises, and meditations were apparent to our clients and staff after just the first session. I highly recommend Miriam's Reaching New Heights Through Health and Happiness to anyone seeking to enhance their ability to enjoy life's blessings."
— Gedale Fenster, Founder, Evolutions Treatment Center

"Miriam has freely shared her prolific educational and spiritual materials with Jewish Girls Unite at retreats and online, giving the girls a new appreciation for prayer and meditation. Her Reaching New Heights series is an incredible resource that offers inspiration, the gift of prayer and meditation, and the secrets to health and happiness."
— Nechama Laber, Jewish Girls Unite

"Miriam Yerushalmi is a very successful therapist and an expert on meditation. At SPARKS, she has helped women healing from Post-Partum Depression and similar mood disorders, enabling them to rebuild their self-image and reconcile past traumas. I endorse and applaud Miriam's Reaching New Heights series for teaching these valuable brain training techniques."
— Esther Kenigsberg, Founder and President, SPARKS

"Mrs. Yerushalmi's unique approach is a beautiful blend of her Chassidic insight and her understanding of human nature. Her ability to see things from a deeper perspective enables her to guide her clients into improving their personal lives in the most challenging of situations."
— Rabbi Shloma Majeski, Dean Machon L'Yahadus; author, The Chassidic Approach to Joy

"The Reaching New Heights series helps connect the seemingly disconnected dots that allow for a clearer picture of yourself, your relation-ships, and ultimately, of your best life."
— Judith Leventhal, CSW, co-author, Small Miracles series

"In her Reaching New Heights series, Miriam thoughtfully tackles universal topics of emotional health. I look forward to recommending her books to my clients and their families!"
— Sharleen Ijadi, Certified Health & Wellness coach

בס"ד

INTRODUCTION

This book is meant for everyone. The information and strategies that it provides were tested over the past three decades in my work as a marriage and family counselor. They have helped couples preparing for marriage as well as married couples whose relationships were at risk. Moreover, they have helped strengthen happy marriages.

As the Lubavitcher Rebbe, Rabbi Menachem Mendel Schneerson, used to say, "Good is good, but better is better."

Marriage can be as holy as a "devouring fire," full of fervor, passion, and enthusiasm. Each spouse can connect with the other and feel such a love for the other that their unity creates within them the most eternal peace on earth, an internal serenity that manifests externally in all their ways.

This true love experience ignites a soul ascent, eager to capture the rapture of Oneness; unifying each other wherever they might be, near or far, always close in heart and soul, until together they are able to conquer worlds, to make an abode for divinity here on earth; to build a true home out of that beautiful love, a miniature sanctuary of their own.

I pray as you read this book that you see the holiness in yourselves and in your spouse, and that you experience much delight all the days of your life, forever together, reaching new heights.

Even husbands and wives who feel that something is amiss in their marriages can reach these heights. Perhaps the relationship has no open conflict, but it is just not the bastion of companionship, warmth, and security they each had dreamed of.

Over time, a relationship may become characterized by lashing out and defensive reactions as husband and wife erect emotional walls, either to hide behind or to keep the other out. All too often, this behavior leads a couple to resign themselves to an unhappy or unfulfilling marriage.

Under such circumstances it is difficult enough to maintain love for oneself, let alone to maintain feelings of love for a spouse who is seen as exacerbating one's pain, if not as the source of it.

How did two people who together have the potential for unity, fall into such a situation?

More importantly, how can peace and love develop in homes and hearts that are surrounded by negativity?

Simply put, the answer to the latter question is, "with kindness." Kindness is the bridge over which you can travel from pain to peace, from shouting to sensitivity.

Kindness can bridge any distance between you and your spouse, or between you and the person you wish to be. Treating yourself, your spouse, and the others in your life with kindness is the first and most important step toward saving your relationships.

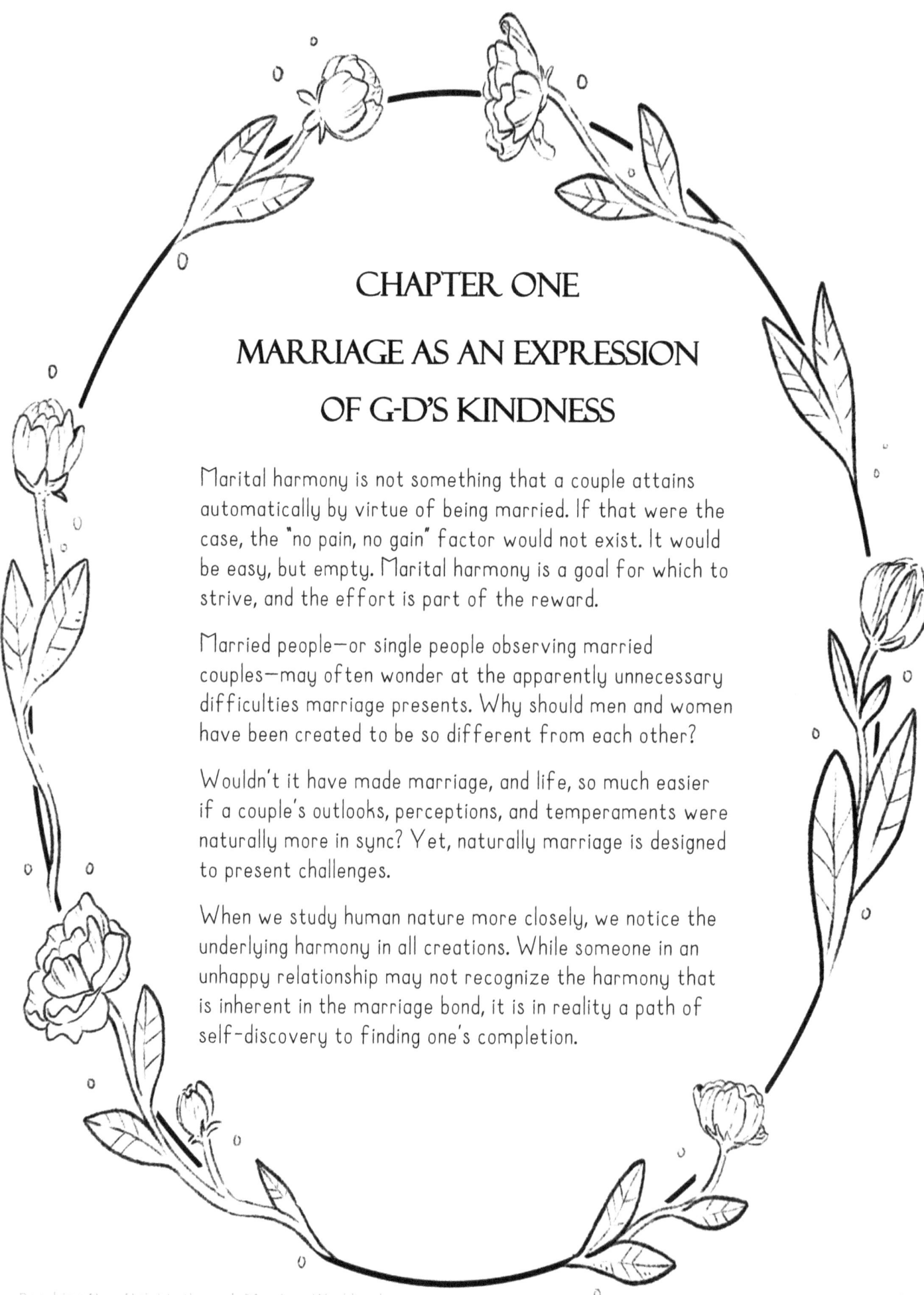

CHAPTER ONE
MARRIAGE AS AN EXPRESSION OF G-D'S KINDNESS

Marital harmony is not something that a couple attains automatically by virtue of being married. If that were the case, the "no pain, no gain" factor would not exist. It would be easy, but empty. Marital harmony is a goal for which to strive, and the effort is part of the reward.

Married people—or single people observing married couples—may often wonder at the apparently unnecessary difficulties marriage presents. Why should men and women have been created to be so different from each other?

Wouldn't it have made marriage, and life, so much easier if a couple's outlooks, perceptions, and temperaments were naturally more in sync? Yet, naturally marriage is designed to present challenges.

When we study human nature more closely, we notice the underlying harmony in all creations. While someone in an unhappy relationship may not recognize the harmony that is inherent in the marriage bond, it is in reality a path of self-discovery to finding one's completion.

Progress generally is not linear.

The time has come to delve into the inner work that will help you keep your relationship healthy by keeping the love within your marriage thriving. This process is not easy, as intimate relationships are inherently challenging. The process of improving the way you relate to your spouse may be fraught with difficulty.

Progress generally is not linear. One day you may feel as if you are soaring toward perfection in your relationship; the next day, you may feel that you are backsliding far and fast.

But strengthening your marriage is a goal that is well worth the struggle.

POINTS FOR PRACTICAL REFLECTIONS

- The Torah views marriage as leading to love, as opposed to the secular view that love leads to marriage.

- The different temperaments of husband and wife demonstrate the infinite aspect of their one soul.

- Like Adam and Chavah, you and your spouse were chosen by Hashem to be partners.

- Every husband and wife, like Yitzchak and Rivkah, have different strengths to contribute to a marriage. These strengths are meant to complement each other and are necessary to achieve your shared goal of building a successful, happy Torah home.

- The challenges of your relationship were designed by G-d specifically to strengthen your marriage.

- Feeling unhappy or disappointed with your spouse does not mean that you married the wrong person.

- Tension in your marriage is a cue that you should work to reveal your love for yourself, your spouse, and Hashem.

EXERCISES

In this chapter we introduce the idea of guided imagery or visualization. Visualization can be a potent tool for personal growth. We each possess an immense ability to train our brain to get in the habit of positive responses. As with any other muscle, exercising your brain increases its capacity over time; the more you use imagery the more your brain grows accustomed to it.

Some people are naturally adept at imagery, but don't worry if your first attempts don't seem effective; most people require time and practice to master it. Persevere, and eventually you will be able to incorporate into your daily routine the behavioral changes that you are targeting.

Visualization can be done anywhere, although it is best done in quiet surroundings where you are not likely to be interrupted.

Sit upright, as that position is most conducive to clear thinking.

The chair should be supportive and allow your feet to touch the floor. Sitting in a recliner may help you to relax, but avoid overstuffed ones and do not recline so far that you relax to the point of falling asleep.

Close your eyes, take a deep breath or two, and try to clear both your mind and your muscles of tension as much as possible. At first you may feel even more stressed at the thought of "forcing" yourself to relax, but this will pass with time and practice.

Then, orchestrate a video in your head of specific scenarios in your life. Picture yourself modeling the behavior you desire to achieve.

For example, visualize a scenario in which you respond to your spouse in a calm and loving manner.

Mentally rehearsing repeatedly the successful outcome that you want to achieve in your life will have a profound impact on your attitudes and reactions.

The sustained concentration you gain from these exercises will improve your abilities in all areas.

During your visualizations, you may examine your relationship with your spouse, perhaps utilizing the following suggestions:

Visualize your soul within you.
See it as one half of a whole.

Visualize your soul as seeking completion. Then look at or visualize your spouse, but see beyond the physical: visualize the other part of your soul *within* your spouse. Finally, visualize the two halves uniting.

Consider the differences between you and your spouse.

Reframe in a positive way any negative view you may have of these differences. If one of you is serious while the other is lighthearted, rather than say, "He/She never takes anything seriously!" or "He/She just has no sense of humor!" say, "Isn't it great that he/she can see the humor in this situation?" or, "My spouse always treats every situation with respect."

Commend yourself for having taken the first step toward improving your marriage.

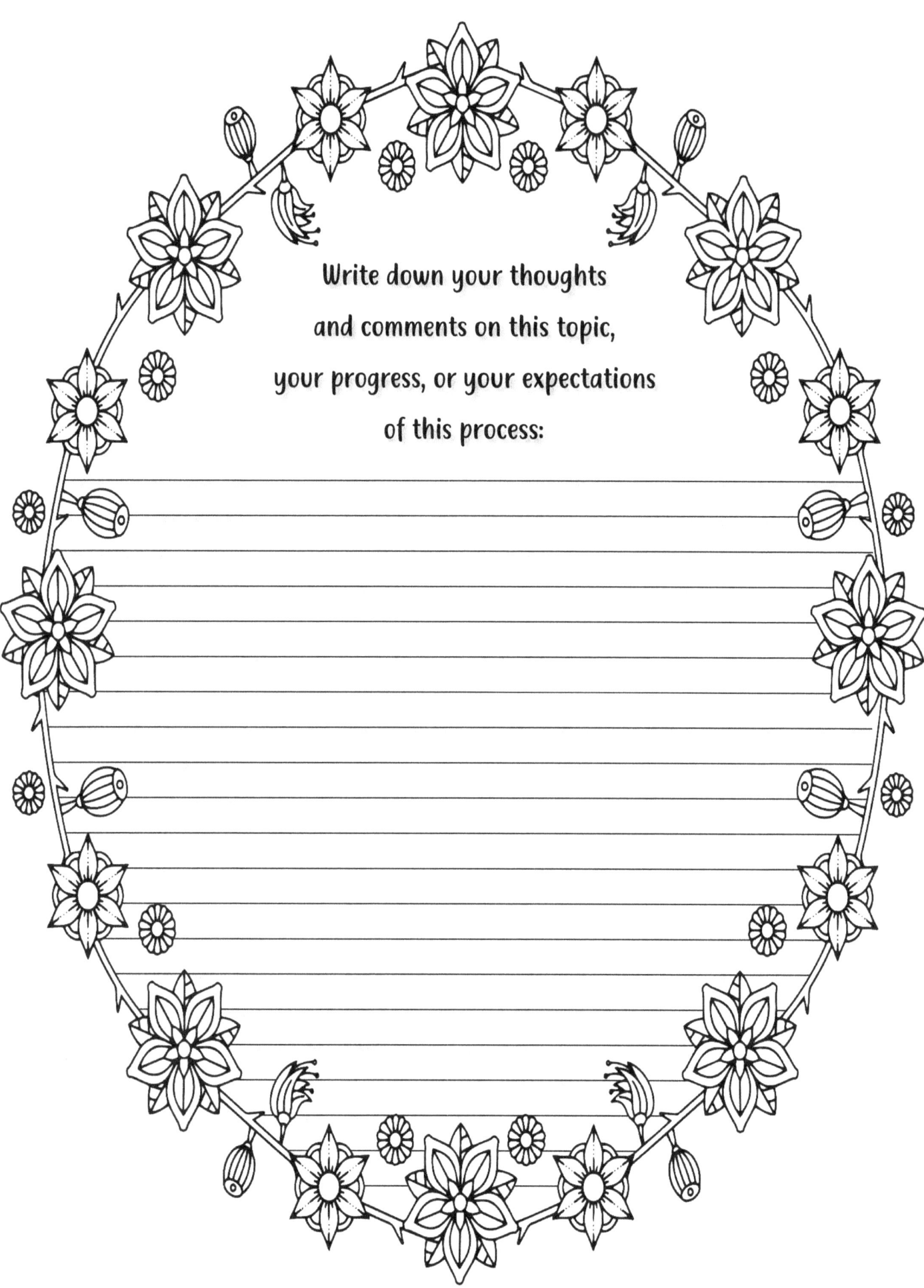

SONG

I am your beloved spouse, the one you can trust.
Like a flower blooming in the bright sunshine,
You are my shield. I'll be yours too.
You are my joy, like a rainbow emerging from the rain.
You are my body and soul, a haven for good.
We will walk through our old days together,
Forever in peace, harmony, and joy.

REFLECTION

What are some common daily events that try your patience?
What is a signal you can use to remind yourself
to practice your quality of patience?

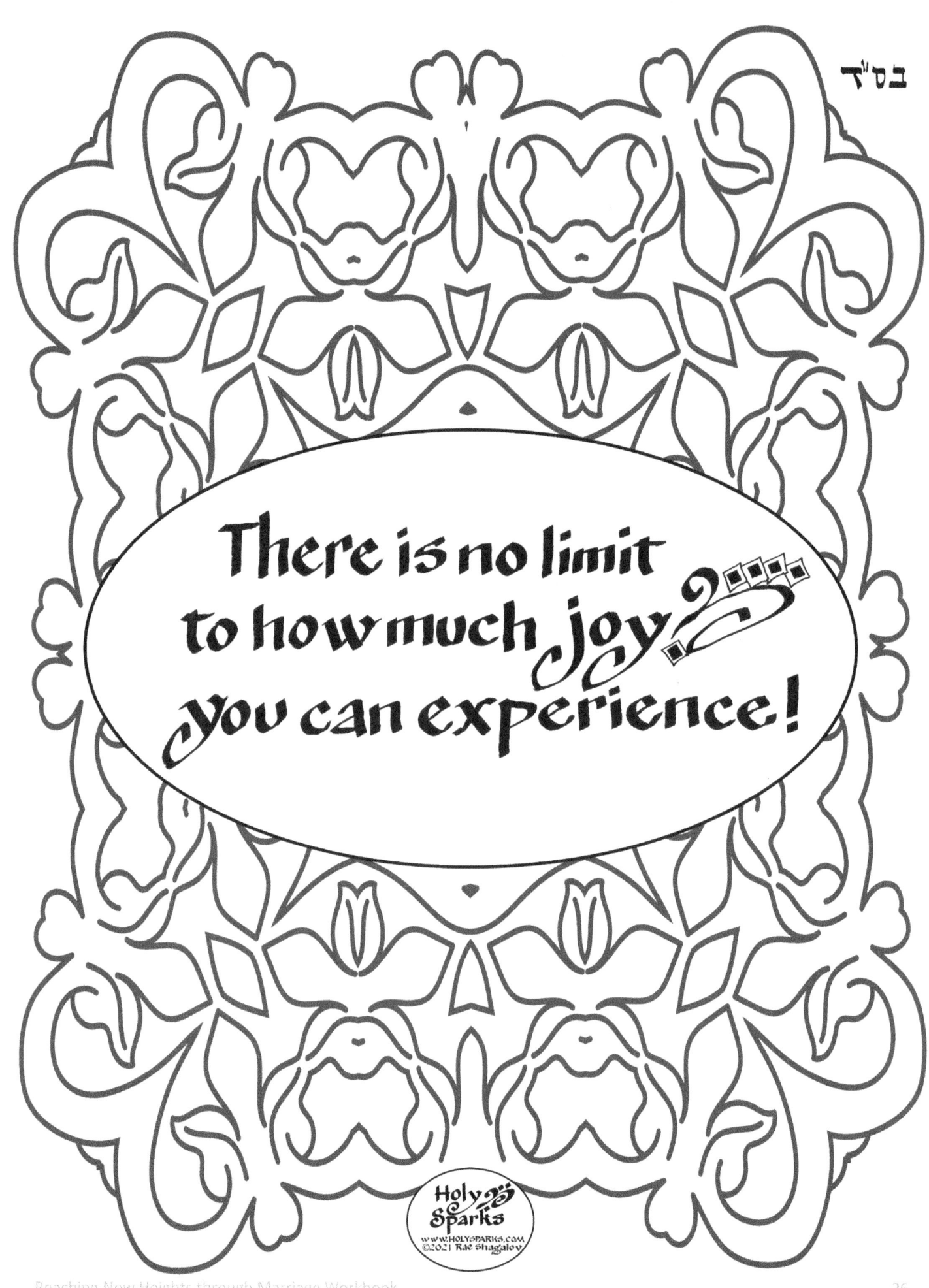

בס"ד

PUT YOUR IMAGINATION TO WORK FOR YOUR MARRIAGE

Don't worry about what is going on in other people's minds; try to control what goes on in your own mind.

The Lubavitcher Rebbe writes:[1]

A Jewish marriage is called a binyan adei ad, "an everlasting edifice." This means that the Jewish home and married life must be built and structured on the foundations of Torah and mitzvos, as emphasized by our sages, whose saintliness was matched by their true wisdom.

The metaphor is meaningful in that when it comes to laying the foundation of a building, it is of no concern what neighbors or passers-by might think of the outer attractiveness of the foundation, much less what scoffers might say about it.

What is important is that the foundation be of tested and durable material that can withstand any erosive elements, and that it be strong enough to support the upper floors that will be added to it.

According to Jewish philosophy, G-d created the world and its inhabitants using four elements (corresponding to the four letters of G-d's holy name): earth, fire, water, and air. Understanding these elements can help us understand human nature.[2]

---

[1] Schneerson, *Letters from the Rebbe* vol. 4, page 151.

[2] For further insight into the elements as they relate to personality, see my book *Let's Go Camping*, as well as my CD, "The Four Elements and You".

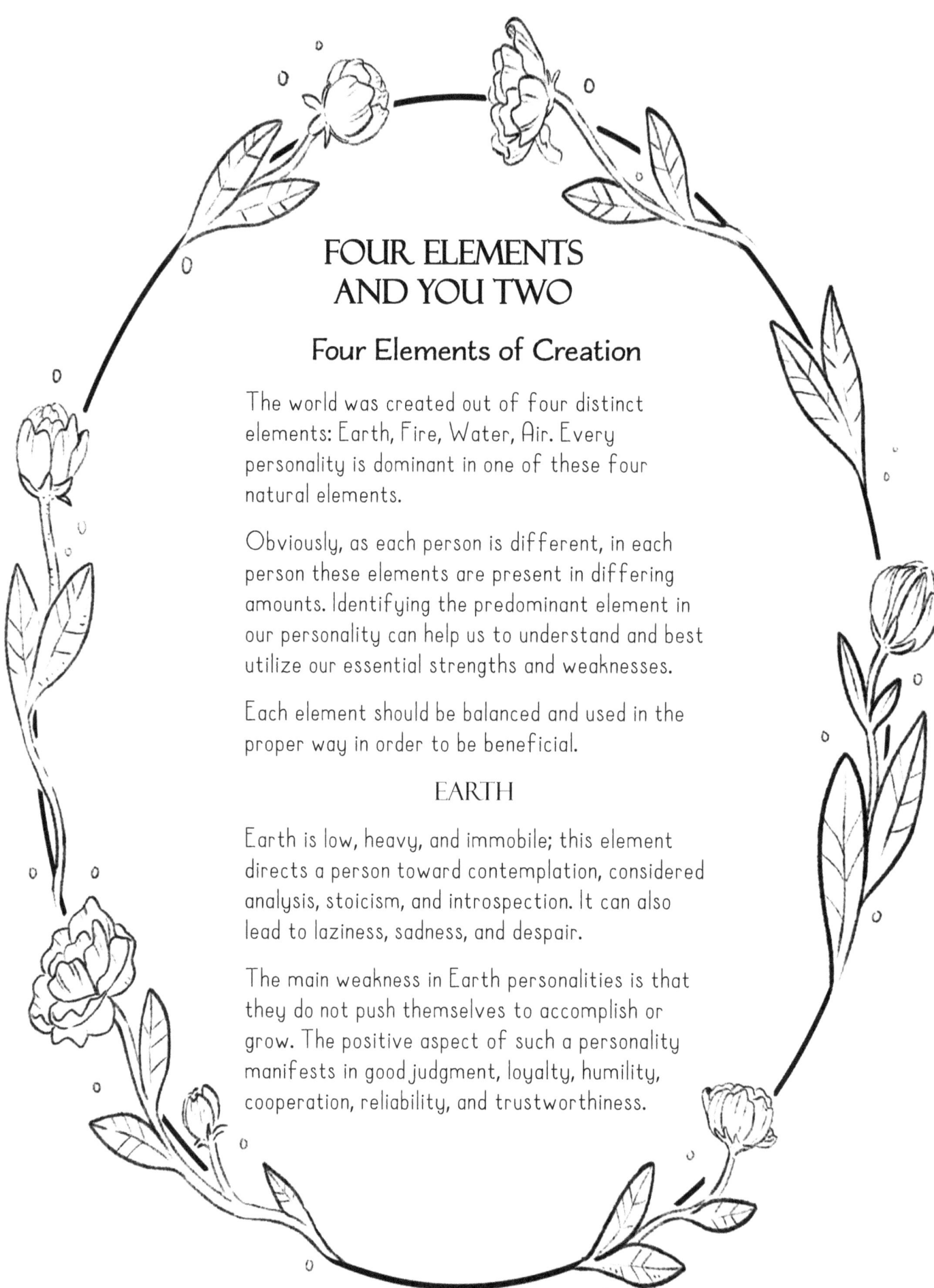

FOUR ELEMENTS AND YOU TWO

Four Elements of Creation

The world was created out of four distinct elements: Earth, Fire, Water, Air. Every personality is dominant in one of these four natural elements.

Obviously, as each person is different, in each person these elements are present in differing amounts. Identifying the predominant element in our personality can help us to understand and best utilize our essential strengths and weaknesses.

Each element should be balanced and used in the proper way in order to be beneficial.

EARTH

Earth is low, heavy, and immobile; this element directs a person toward contemplation, considered analysis, stoicism, and introspection. It can also lead to laziness, sadness, and despair.

The main weakness in Earth personalities is that they do not push themselves to accomplish or grow. The positive aspect of such a personality manifests in good judgment, loyalty, humility, cooperation, reliability, and trustworthiness.

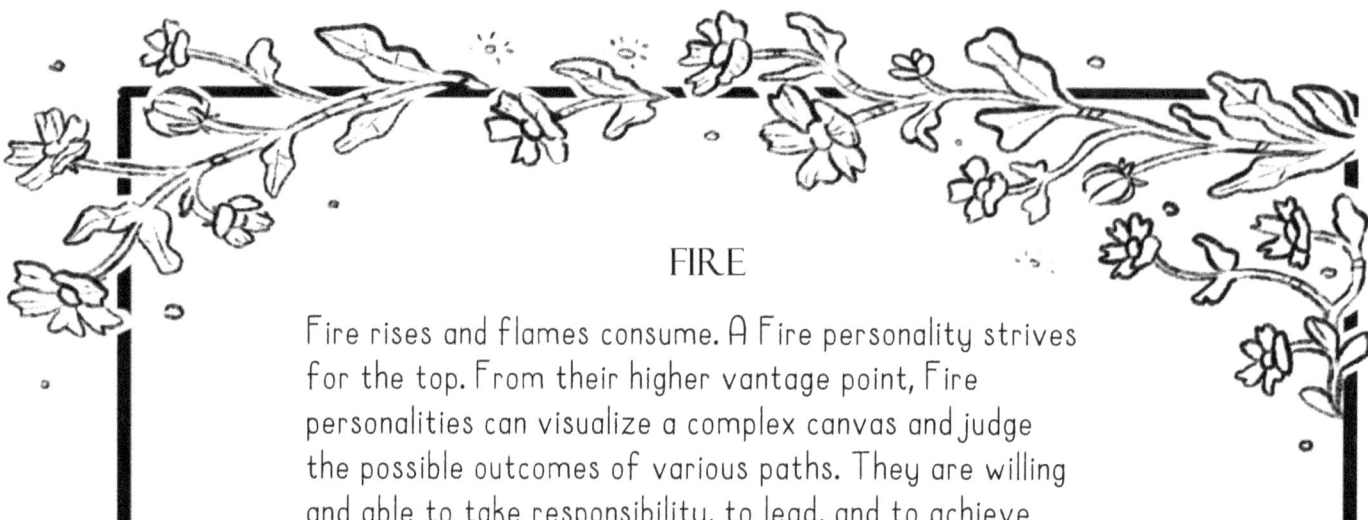

FIRE

Fire rises and flames consume. A Fire personality strives for the top. From their higher vantage point, Fire personalities can visualize a complex canvas and judge the possible outcomes of various paths. They are willing and able to take responsibility, to lead, and to achieve.

The negative expressions of this personality type are the explosive character flaws of arrogance, anger, criticism and condescension toward others; the ability to take control can become an overwhelming desire for power.

On the positive side, Fire can be used to warm one's heart and it can be channeled into serving G-d with a fiery passion; Fire personalities can reach great heights of spiritual loftiness, wisdom, and success.

WATER

Water has no innate boundaries; it must be contained by an external receptacle. A Water person "goes with the flow," spreading out wherever access leads. They are easygoing and loving, able to give of themselves and to help others grow.

The negative manifestations of a Water personality may be instability, a lack of self-control, and a lack of judgment; following the path of least resistance often leads to a life of physical excess and addictions.

Water-dominant people, never feeling they have enough, have a need to amass possessions. This desire can be channeled in a positive way towards the acquisition of more personal growth and positive accomplishments.

AIR

Air is invisible, everywhere and anywhere, impossible to pin down. An Air person is a wonderful source of ideas and idealism, and yearns to follow the spiritual, transcendent path.

Air-dominant people are not particularly concerned with physical realities or needs. Routine is uncomfortable to them. They may find it difficult to stick with a chosen path, and will flit from one position to another.

An Air person is also very involved with the power of speech, whose source is air. They are able to speak well and convincingly, and can use words in holy ways to help others—e.g., as teachers, clergy, therapists—but may abuse this ability by speaking aimlessly or harmfully.

Determining which trait defines you or your spouse will take time and careful analysis; it may not be obvious which trait predominates. In some people, two or more traits may be equally dominant. Knowing one's tendencies, though, makes it easier to deal with and direct them. Once you understand your character, you will be better able to refine it.

POINTS FOR PRACTICAL REFLECTIONS

- The goal of a married couple is to regain that level of unity they had in heaven.

- When we strive to achieve that unity, G-d helps us also achieve the personal transformation to which we aspire.

- Improving our character will improve our relationships.

- It is possible to change our instincts and patterns.

- A bamboo plant takes years to grow roots, but the plant flourishes to great heights in weeks.

- Be patient with yourself and those you love.

- We may turn to G-d for all our needs, material and spiritual.

- We may have absolute faith that with G-d's help we will achieve our goal.

- Focused *tefillah*, prayer, expands our mind and refines our emotions.

- Four different elements, in infinite combination, form the basis of our personality.

- Determining the dominant element in our personality helps us to know our strengths and weaknesses.

- Learning Torah helps us rise above the turmoil in our lives.

- Increased *bitachon* makes it easier for you to be patient with yourself and others.

Remember that progress may be slow, but every step counts.

EXERCISES AND MEDITATIONS

Evaluate the expectations you have for yourself. Consider your responsibilities and your available time. Are your expectations realistic? If not, adjust them to your reality.

If necessary, decrease your demands on yourself and place limits on the demands made on you by others.

Accept upon yourself only goals that can actually be accomplished without overwhelming you. If you feel torn between wanting to spend every second of the day with your children and trying to find time to pray, be creative and find ways to fit both into your schedule.

For example, when my children were infants, if I didn't wake up early enough to pray on my own, I would pray with them or I would wait until they napped and finish my prayers at that time.

Once you have set some goals for yourself, note your progress regularly. Remember that progress may be slow, but every step counts.

VISUALIZE

Visualize a baby taking its first steps.

See yourself smiling at the baby's wobbling efforts. See yourself applauding the baby. Notice that the baby seems very satisfied with its progress, and may even applaud its own efforts. It is not discouraged by frequent falls.

Visualize yourself making progress in baby steps. Smile at yourself, as you would smile at a baby.

Applaud yourself—mentally or actually, with some small reward—for your efforts. Be patient with yourself. Do not be discouraged if you falter.

Visualize yourself during *tefillah* **(prayer)** as a car at a gas station, filling up on all three intellectual powers. There is no limit to how much you can take, or to how much Hashem can expand your intelligence and your mindfulness.

Devote some time to determining your predominant characteristic. Be aware that many people have two or even all four elements dominant.

Realize that one trait may be easier to rectify than another, which may require many years of personal work.

Set up a plan to utilize your strengths in your areas of challenge.

(This will be discussed further in the next chapter.)

MEDITATION EXERCISES

Ask yourself, "What element in myself and what element in my spouse makes us susceptible to certain negative traits?"

Imagine different ways in which you could help strengthen yourself and your spouse to overcome those traits.

When the demands upon you seem overwhelming, visualize yourself in an ark, rising safely above the raging waters.

Three exercises can help achieve further expansion of the mind:

1) *Hitbodedut*, **solitude:** training yourself to be alone with Hashem.

2) *Iyun* (or *hitbonenut*), **contemplation:** taking the time to thoroughly investigate and understand what you are learning, through focused review.

3) *Hitakvut*, **deliberation:** focusing your attention on the subject matter to the exclusion of everything else.

The morning is the best time of day to perform any meditative exercise, but maximum concentration at any time will be beneficial.

Merely mouthing the words of *tefillah* or the *Tanya* of the day will not suffice. Reading the words out loud will increase your concentration.

Try to think of the meaning of the words as you say them.

SPEAK TO G-D

For at least five minutes a day, read aloud a portion of the daily prayers or a chapter of Psalms in a language you understand, as though you are speaking to Hashem.

Then, in your own words, tell Hashem about an issue with which you are struggling. Consider the issue from different angles. Focus only on one issue at a time.

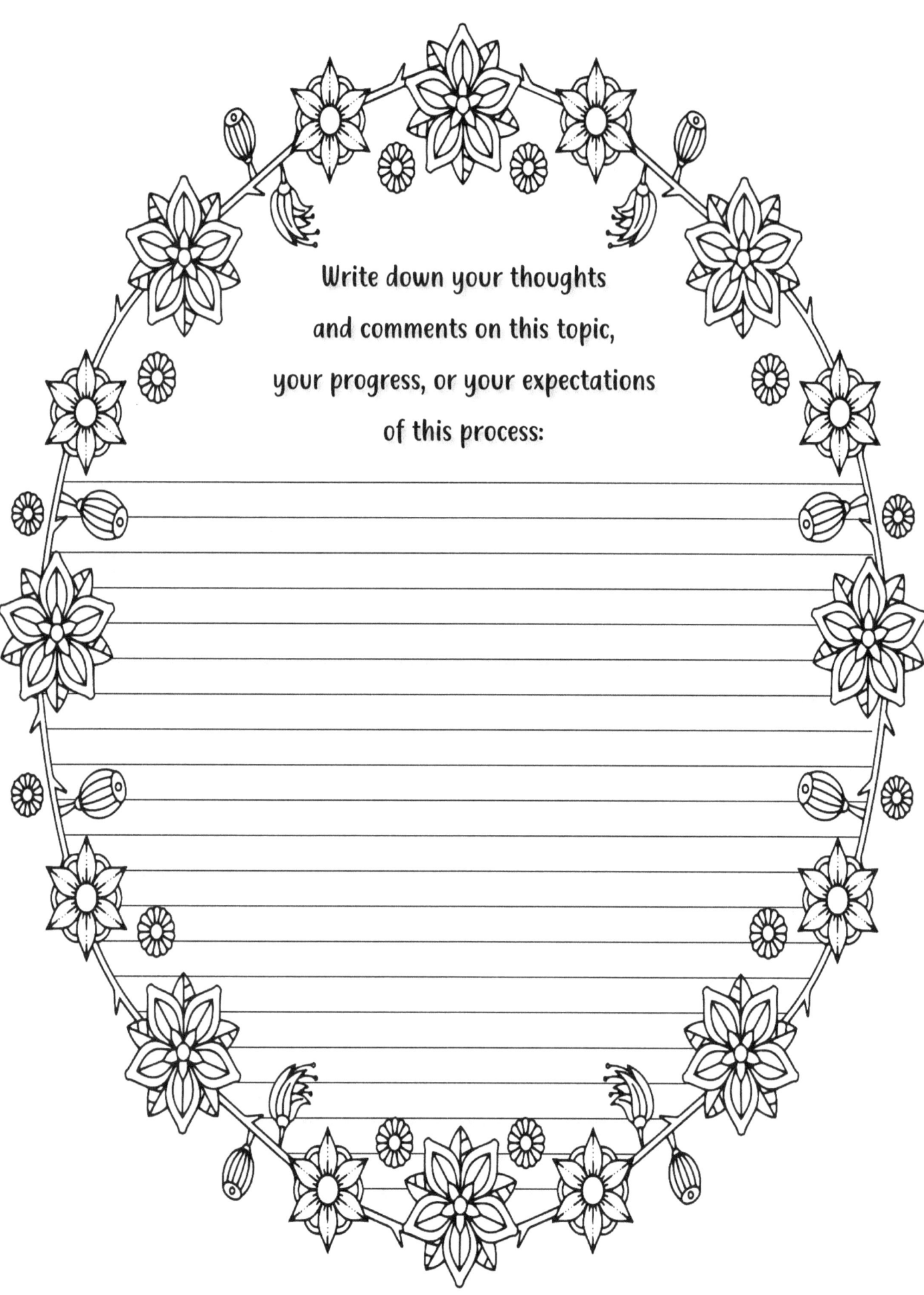

Write down your thoughts and comments on this topic, your progress, or your expectations of this process:

בס"ד

Chapter Three

CHAPTER THREE
INTROSPECTION & RESTRAINT

It is common for us to note the flaws of others. It may be less common to notice our own flaws. Very often, although we may be reluctant to admit it, the flaws we are noticing in others mirror the very characteristics or habits we dislike in ourselves. In order to effect beneficial change, we have to strive to accept human imperfections.

Fortunately, we have the ability to perceive any person—including ourselves and our spouses—and any situation in a positive way. Maintain a high level of self-awareness, and, after determining your dominant personality trait (as discussed in the preceding chapter), utilize it for good.

POINTS FOR PRACTICAL REFLECTIONS

- Often the fault you find in others, may be your own.

- Recognizing and trying to correct your own character flaws increases your patience for others and their flaws.

- Realize that every negative attribute is simply an unrectified positive attribute.

- Be honest but compassionate when you examine your faults.

- If you can love yourself despite your imperfections, you can love your spouse despite his or her imperfections.

- Your efforts at self-improvement will influence your spouse to make positive changes as well.

- Negative character traits can be seen as indications of one's high-level soul and the potential spiritual heights one can attain.

- Accepting criticism calmly and thoughtfully reduces the likelihood of being criticized in the future.

- Silence is sometimes the best response.

EXERCISES AND MEDITATIONS

Recognize the positive in yourself: Write down three positive qualities you have. Recall the positive effect utilizing those qualities has on those around you. Then write down three positive qualities you wish you had.

Visualize yourself possessing those qualities. Visualize yourself acting in a manner consistent with those positive traits.

Visualize the positive effect mastering those qualities can have on your life.

Now consider that your spouse possesses positive qualities that complement your own. Acknowledge the positive qualities your spouse possesses, and the beneficial effects that accompany them. Write them down.

Then write down three positive qualities you wish your spouse possessed. Visualize him or her mastering those qualities and acting in a manner consistent with those positive traits.

Visualize the positive effect that could have on your life together.

Strive to accept imperfections in yourself and your spouse.

Identify a negative character trait that you possess and one that your spouse possesses.

Envision yourself applying this trait in a positive way.

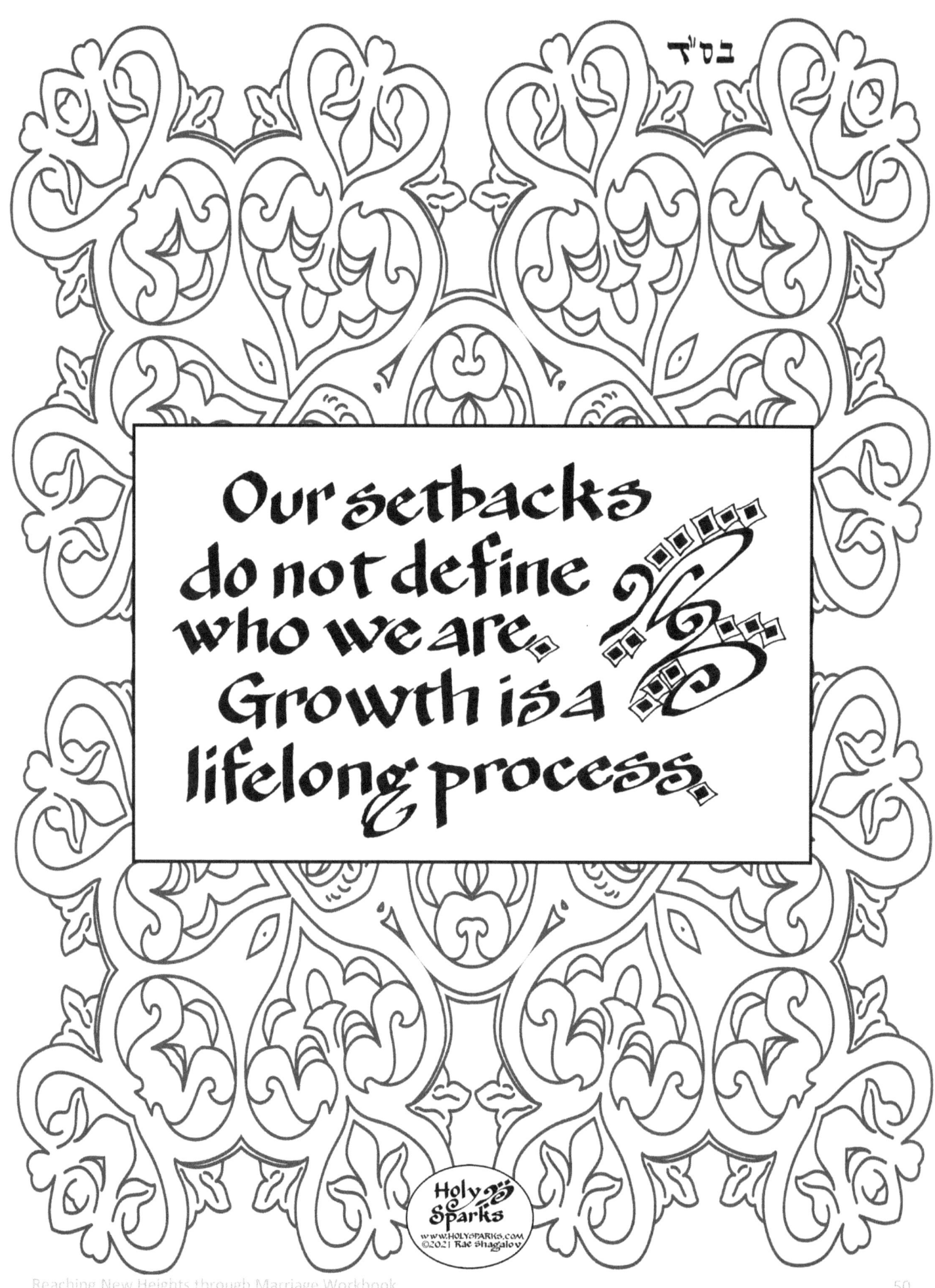

Your efforts at self-improvement will influence your spouse to make positive changes as well.

Map out the steps you think would be necessary for you to make that happen.

Increase your awareness of how your speech might be contributing to tension in your marital relationship.

Ask yourself questions such as, "Did I speak in a refined manner today? Did I get anxious when my spouse seemed angry or critical with me? Was I spiteful? Did I sound condescending?"

Note the instances in which you restrained yourself from an angry, impulsive, or critical comment.

Note the positive effects this restraint engendered—even if they seem minimal.

You may want to keep a written record of these instances.

Write down your thoughts and comments on this topic, your progress, or your expectations of this process:

_____
_____
_____
_____
_____
_____
_____
_____
_____
_____
_____
_____
_____
_____

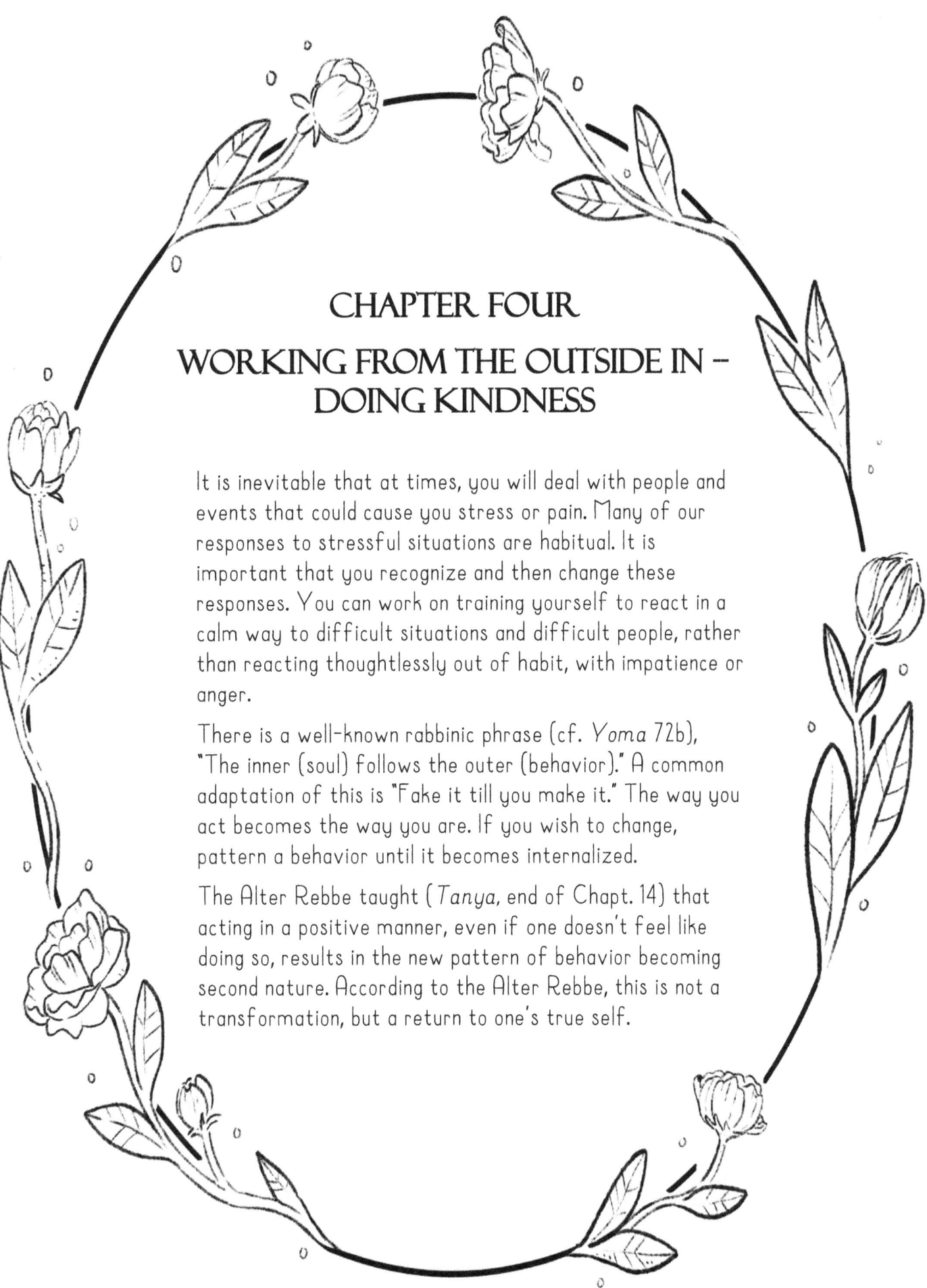

CHAPTER FOUR
WORKING FROM THE OUTSIDE IN – DOING KINDNESS

It is inevitable that at times, you will deal with people and events that could cause you stress or pain. Many of our responses to stressful situations are habitual. It is important that you recognize and then change these responses. You can work on training yourself to react in a calm way to difficult situations and difficult people, rather than reacting thoughtlessly out of habit, with impatience or anger.

There is a well-known rabbinic phrase (cf. *Yoma* 72b), "The inner (soul) follows the outer (behavior)." A common adaptation of this is "Fake it till you make it." The way you act becomes the way you are. If you wish to change, pattern a behavior until it becomes internalized.

The Alter Rebbe taught (*Tanya*, end of Chapt. 14) that acting in a positive manner, even if one doesn't feel like doing so, results in the new pattern of behavior becoming second nature. According to the Alter Rebbe, this is not a transformation, but a return to one's true self.

POINTS FOR PRACTICAL REFLECTIONS

- The way you act influences the way you are.
- Acting kind leads to being kind.
- A pleasant expression leads to a pleasant disposition.
- Smiles given usually result in smiles returned.
- Verbalizing emotions intensifies the emotion.
- Speaking kindly leads to feeling kind. Speaking lovingly leads to feelings of love.
- Being nice to your spouse increases your compassion, which increases the positive energy in your marriage.
- Acting kindly to your spouse is a mitzvah and thus confers tremendous spiritual benefits on you.
- Rebuke must be motivated by the true desire to help your spouse or your efforts will be dismissed simply as criticism.
- Providing some tangible benefit to your partner before proferring criticism renders the rebuke more acceptable.
- Offering criticism calmly and patiently mitigates its sting.
- Excessive criticism may spring from low self-esteem.
- Learning Torah is a cure for low self-esteem.
- Learning Torah connects your soul to G-d.
- Learning Torah with your spouse connects your two souls together.

EXERCISES AND MEDITATIONS

Practice acts of kindness toward your spouse. Try to predict his or her needs before he or she expresses them. For example, if your spouse likes a cup of tea or coffee in the morning, try to have one ready when he or she wakes up. Offer it with a smile and a pleasant "Good morning." Or, if your spouse is entering the house laden with packages, stop what you are doing to help. As you do so, greet your spouse pleasantly and with a smile.

If you can afford it, get household help. The Lubavitcher Rebbe was once asked if folding one's *tallis* (prayer shawl) right after Shabbos is a *segulah* (a good omen) for *shalom bayis*. The Rebbe replied that helping clean the dishes is a better *segulah*.

Compliment your spouse often, even for small and ordinary acts. When you offer such a compliment, smile warmly and speak lovingly, even if that means exaggerating. The Talmud (*Kesuvos* 111b) tells us, "It is better to show your white teeth to your friend than to serve him milk." That is, a smile and words of encouragement often benefit a person more than material assistance can.

Visualize yourself in a situation to which you usually respond with anger or impatience, and with a frown or scowl upon your face. Now visualize yourself responding with a smile and kind words.

Practice a pleasant expression in front of a mirror until you become used to it. Visualize yourself maintaining this pleasant expression throughout various interactions with your spouse.

To inspire yourself to act kindly toward your spouse, consider that although Achitofel taught King David only two things[3], King David remained so grateful that even after Achitofel turned against him he accorded him great respect, referring to him as his teacher, guide, and intimate[4].

Focus on two occasions on which your spouse has done a beneficial action for you. Perhaps he or she assisted you with some difficult chore (albeit with some negative comments), gave you an unexpected compliment, or even surprised you with a small but thoughtful gift. Perhaps he or she simply did not do a negative action when you were expecting one. For these reasons alone, you can thank your spouse sincerely and praise him or her for the effort (or the restraint).

Establish a regular time of Torah study for yourself, and encourage your spouse to do so as well. Be sure only to encourage and not to pressure.

Establish a regular period of Torah study for you and your spouse together.

Say "I love you" to your spouse, often. Even though at first doing so may feel forced, eventually you will find that your feelings match your words.

---

[3]Achitofel taught King David 1) to study Torah with a partner, for only then would the learning endure, and 2) to run to prayer like a person following the king. *Kallah Rabbasi* 8.

[4]See *Rashi* on *Pirkei Avos* 6:2.

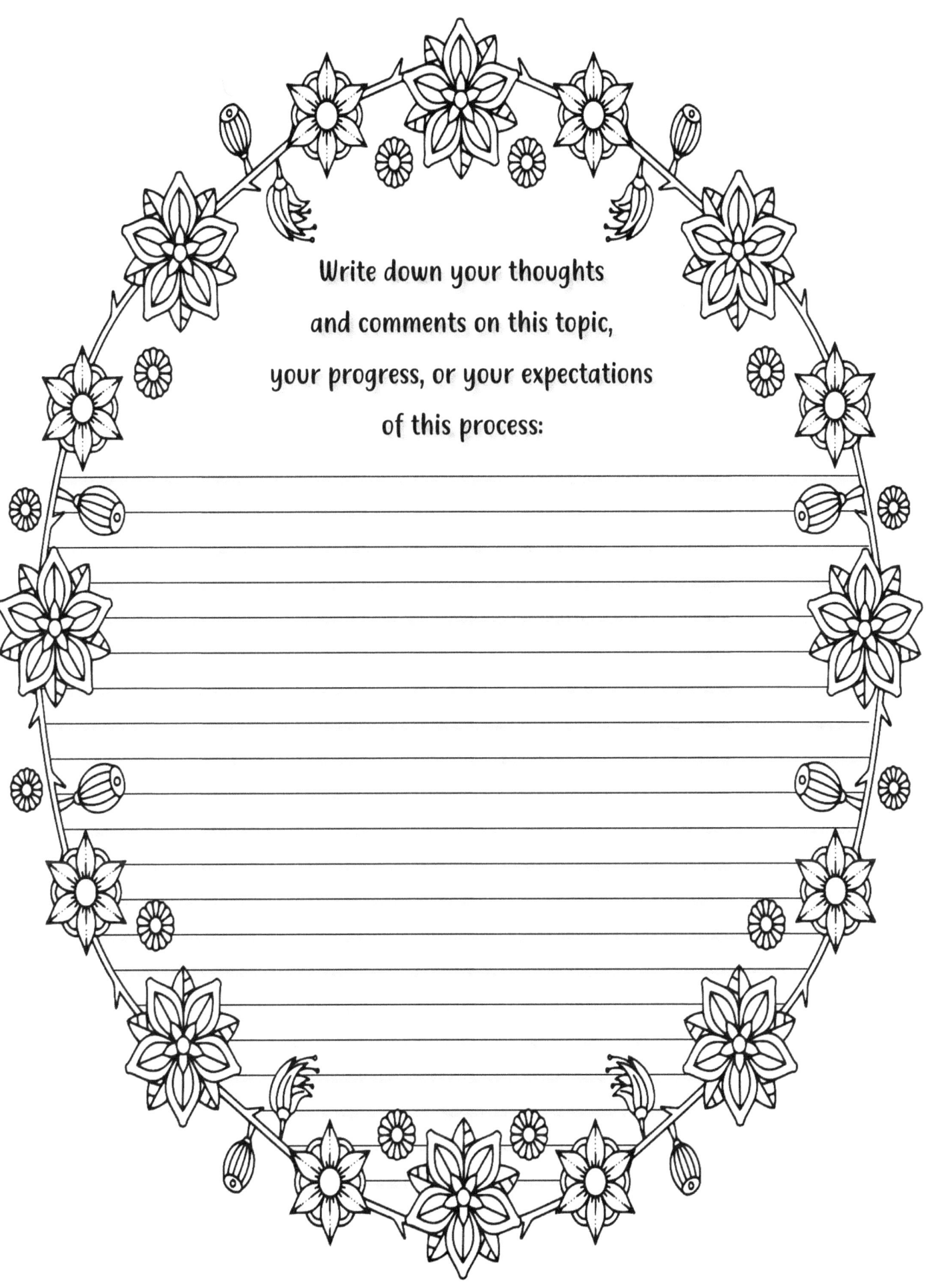

Write down your thoughts and comments on this topic, your progress, or your expectations of this process:

CHAPTER FIVE
WORKING FROM THE INSIDE OUT – YOU THINK, YOU CAN

Once we have begun to work on our physical behavior, the next step is to work on our mental behavior. The Alter Rebbe teaches that we definitely have the ability, as well as the responsibility, to control and direct our thoughts to the good:[5]

[M]an was so created from birth, that every person may, with the power of the will in his brain—i.e., the will created of his mind's understanding—restrain himself and control the drive of his heart's lust, preventing his heart's desires from finding expression in deed, word, and thought, and [he can, if his mind wills it,] divert his attention completely from that which his heart craves [and turn his attention] to the exact opposite direction.

The Rebbe[6] based this teaching on the verse (Gen. 37:24) describing the pit that Joseph's brothers threw Joseph into as "empty, there was no water in it." Rashi comments that the pit was dry and empty of water, but it was filled with snakes and scorpions. The Torah is compared to water, and if one's mind and heart are empty of the water of Torah, they will instead be filled with the "snakes and scorpions" of negativity, aimlessness, evil thoughts, and depression.

It will be much easier for your mind to affect your character when you fill your mind with Torah. However, the Rebbe Rashab points out that many people learn Torah but do not change their character traits. What does work to change one's *middos* is meditative prayer, when one concentrates with deep contemplation on the words of the *tefillos* and their meanings, and on Hashem's wisdom and greatness in conjunction with prayer. Through meditative prayer, one draws Hashem's light into his or her mind and changes the actual physical structure of the brain.

---

[5] *Likkutei Amarim*, vol 1, chap. 12, pages 176-177.

[6] *Likkutei Sichot: Vayechi.*

POINTS FOR PRACTICAL REFLECTIONS

- We have the ability to control and direct our thoughts.

- Reprogramming habitual responses takes repeated efforts and much time, but perseverance brings about change.

- The desire to attain holiness is the most powerful motivation for change, but mundane purposes will also work.

- Praying and learning Torah should be the first steps that you take to gain self-control.

- Praying and learning Torah increases our own Divine wisdom.

- Meditating on Hashem's wisdom and greatness draws Hashem's light into our mind and changes the actual physical structure of the brain.

- It is easier to change our intellectual awareness than to directly change our character traits.

- A positive outlook leads to a positive outcome.

- One is not responsible for negative thoughts that come to mind spontaneously, but one *is* responsible for what is done with those thoughts.

- Negative thoughts create a barrier between you and others.

- *Teshuvah* can break down the barrier of negativity.

- You may not be able to control other people or situations, but you can always control your attitude.

EXERCISES AND MEDITATIONS

Visualize yourself beginning a new, healthy habit. Imagine this habit being engraved into the grooves of your brain. Then visualize your brain building a "wiring" system that connects it to your heart, until you feel empowered to achieve.

Imagine yourself driving a powerful car which can only be controlled through your thoughts. You know it is imperative to keep the vehicle from exceeding a certain speed in order to avoid a destructive crash or collision. You direct all your mental energy toward keeping the car running smoothly, adjusting your speed and grip to accommodate the twists and turns of the road, always alert to the possibility of unexpected obstacles. You practice mental control of the vehicle every day, until you become its master.

Designate a set time for Torah learning. Optimally, each session should be no less than 15 minutes, but you may begin at five minutes and gradually increase the duration. During this time, focus only on the Torah topic. If you are interrupted, begin again. It is best to read Torah passages out loud, as this reinforces the learning and serves as an aid in focusing.

Visualize the Torah you are learning as beams of light. Visualize these beams focused on a target. Visualize this light cleansing and healing the targeted area. Finally, visualize G-d's holy light entering and healing your heart and mind and banishing the darkness of the animal soul.

Imagine yourself accompanied by the angels created by your thoughts. Realize that you can surround yourself with positive forces of your own making.

Visualize the angels you have created through your thoughts about your spouse. If necessary, visualize your *teshuvah* dissolving the negative angels around you and your spouse.

Imagine that you are standing next to an artist and admiring her work. You are so impressed by her creative abilities that you gush forth words of praise: "Your hands are golden. It is amazing how you blend those colors. The picture looks so real. You're so talented."

Imagine what pleasure the artist receives from these words. In the same way, when you appreciate that you yourself are G-d's handiwork, a Divinely created being fulfilling G-d's will in the world, you give G-d—the Artist—the ultimate pleasure. Imagine how much greater His pleasure will be when you appreciate your spouse and your marriage as His handiwork.

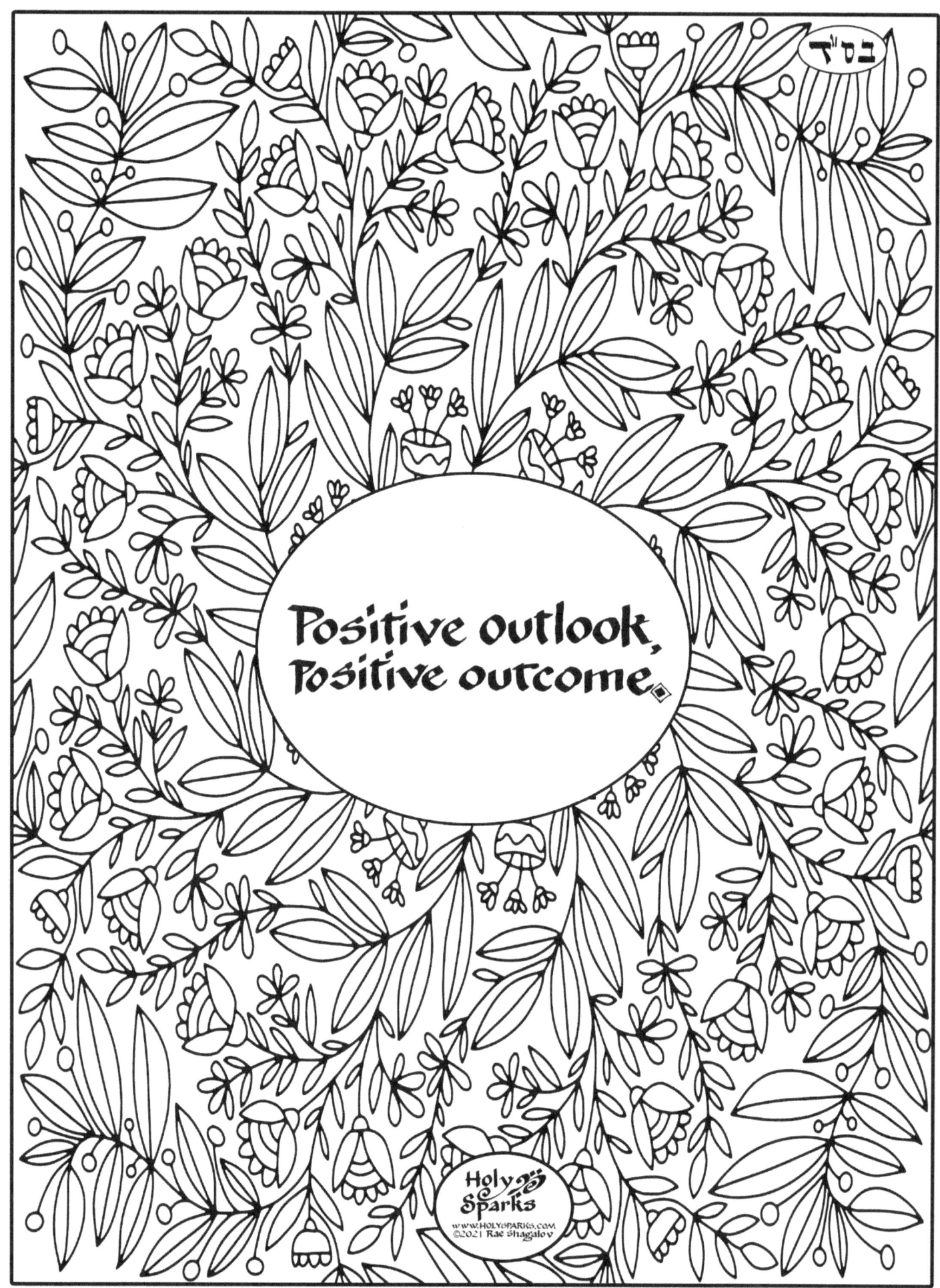

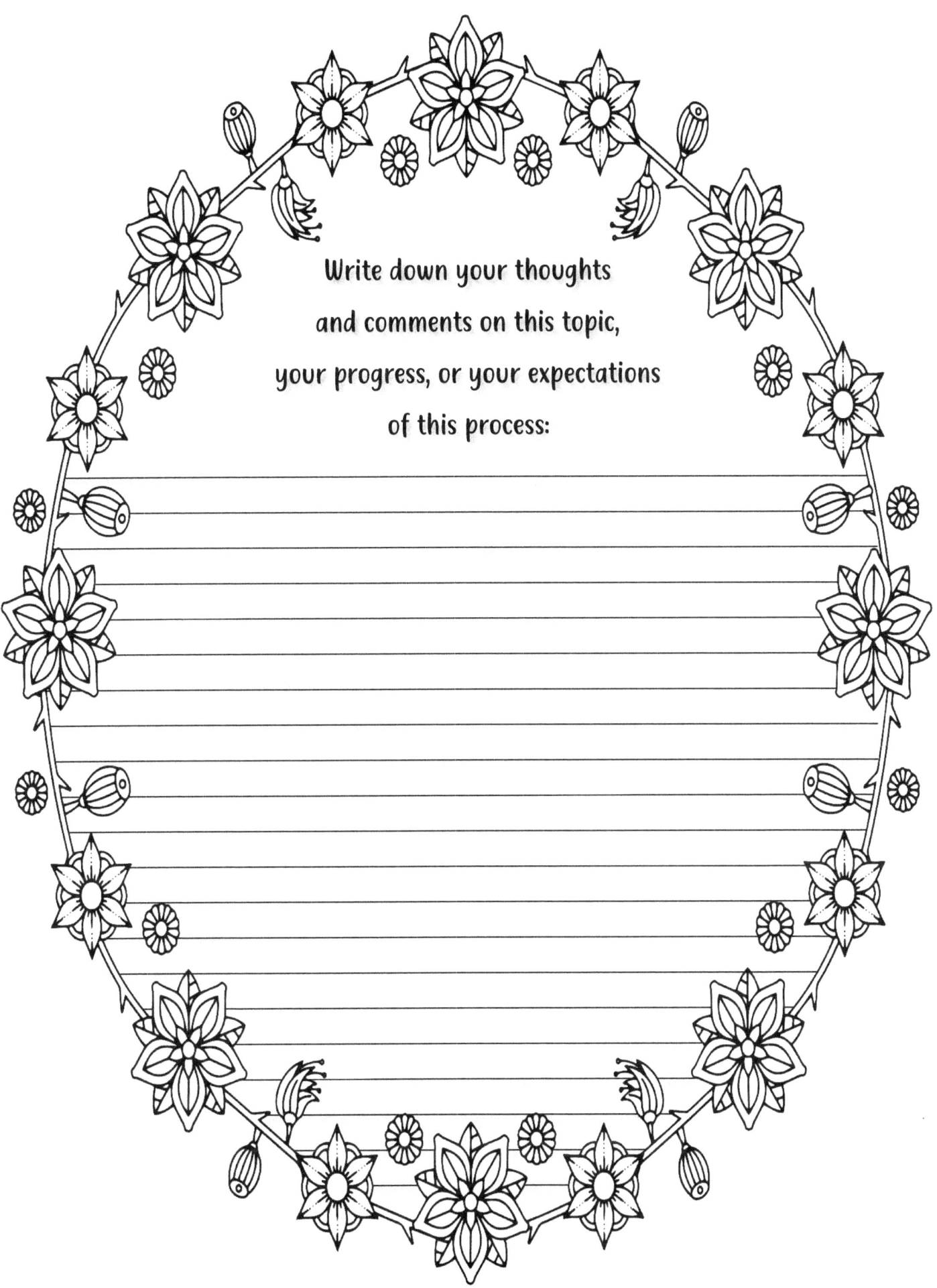

Write down your thoughts and comments on this topic, your progress, or your expectations of this process:

בס"ד

CHAPTER SIX
RESPECT AND HUMILITY

Prayer and Torah learning are essential steps to self-improvement and improved relationships, but they fall primarily into the category of *ben adam lemakom*, "between man and the Creator," our spiritual relationship with Hashem. There is another necessary element, equally important, which comes under the category of *ben adam lechaveiro*, "between man and his fellow man," interpersonal relationships.

"*Derech eretz kadmah leTorah*, respect comes before learning."[7] Treating others with respect is a fundamental element of a Torah life. Without this essential character trait, one cannot fully absorb the Torah's teachings.

The respect that a husband and wife ought to show each other possesses a quality beyond that which we are supposed to accord each other as Jews. Although *shalom bayis* will be benefitted by even that general level of respect, it will be immeasurably strengthened if a couple can reach that higher level specific to spouses.

---

[7] *Midrash Vayikra Rabbah* chap. 9.

POINTS FOR PRACTICAL REFLECTIONS

- Replacing arrogance with humility allows you to treat your spouse respectfully.
- Reciprocity is the key to a harmonious relationship.
- When you give your spouse respect, you elevate your own soul.
- When you strive to make your spouse happy, your spouse will strive to make you happy.
- Judging favorably can prevent unpleasant misunderstandings.
- When you judge others, consider all the factors that have gone into their situation and behavior.
- Behavior you consider to be provocative may actually be only your misinterpretation of the situation.
- Marriage is a partnership and each partner has a distinct role.

Regard your spouse as a rare and precious commodity, made even more valuable by certain singularities of character.

EXERCISES AND MEDITATIONS

Imagine that you possess a rare and precious artifact, made even more valuable by certain irregularities in its finish. These imperfections may be very small but they enhance immeasurably the total worth of the object. Realizing that, you can ignore those imperfections in your regard for the object. You can even develop an appreciation for those very irregularities and the singular value they add. Now, regard your spouse as a rare and precious commodity, made even more valuable by certain singularities of character.

Realize that you have willingly accepted the mission of caring for this precious object. You have the power and the ability to keep this object in good shape and even to increase its value. You also have the capability of destroying it.

Reflect on the fact that if you take proper care of this valuable item, your own value will increase, and in the end its original owner will reward you handsomely; if you destroy it, your own value will correspondingly decrease, and you will have to account for your mishandling of the task.

Visualize your spouse as a member of a royal family who is in exile and unaware of his or her true identity. Consider the great opportunity you have to serve this exalted personage, and how greatly your efforts will be appreciated by him/her and the entire royal family later on, when they are ultimately reunited. Think of how much more you would be willing to do for such a person and how humble you would feel around them in their proper environment.

Realize that as a Jew, the descendent of Abraham, you are able to attain humility, no matter how caught up in arrogance you might be. Gain inspiration from the examples of the self-sacrifice of our Patriarchs and Matriarchs.

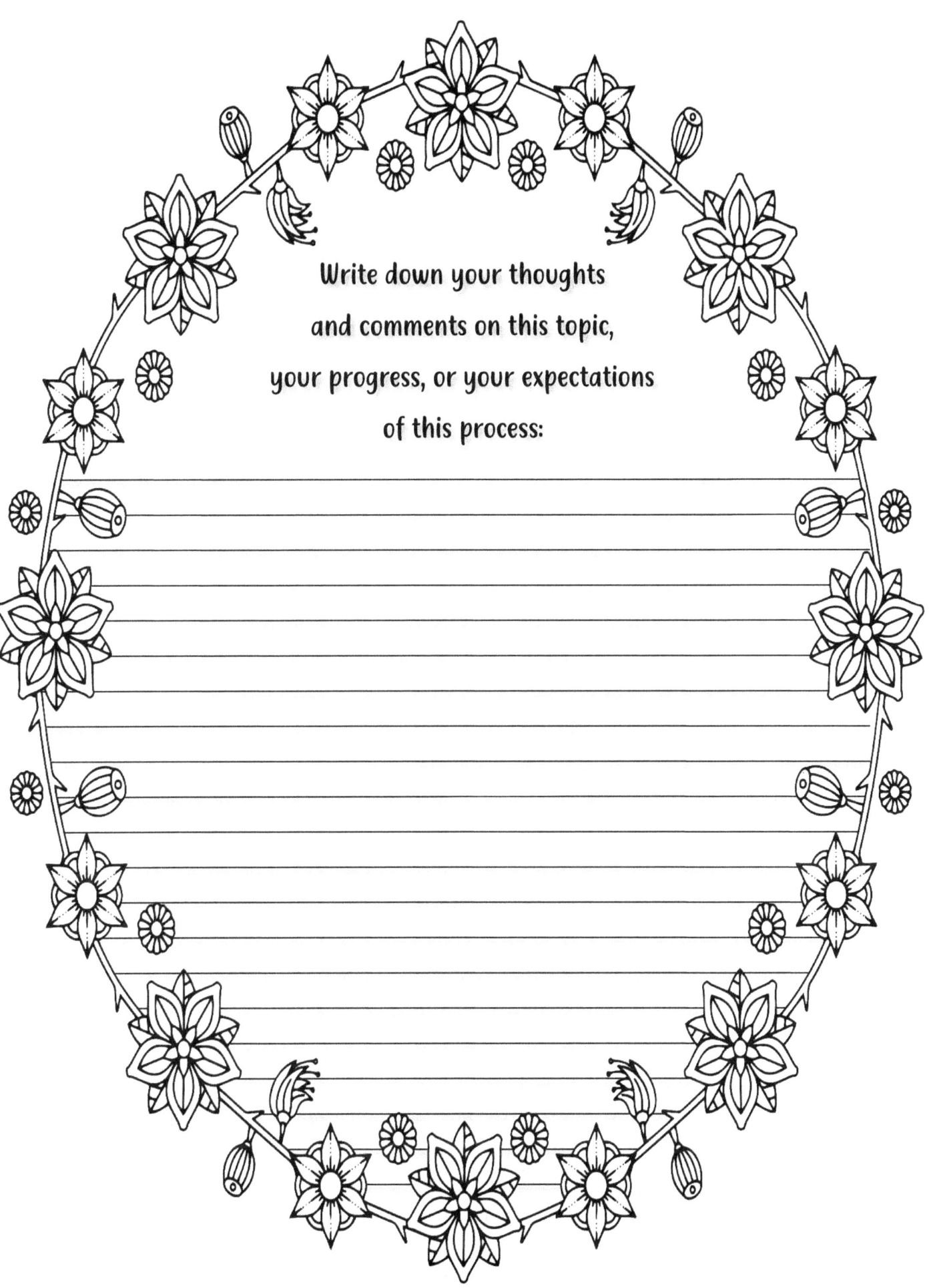

Write down your thoughts and comments on this topic, your progress, or your expectations of this process:

CHAPTER SEVEN
THE ROLE OF WOMEN

The dynamic in which one respects and helps one's spouse and as a result is elevated as well, is particularly germane to women.

The verse describing Miriam as a prophet identifies her only as the sister of Aharon and not as the sister of Moshe (Moses), who was the leader of all Israel and their greatest prophet. Rashi explains that the verse is written this way to teach that Miriam was a prophet even before Moshe was born.

The Lubavitcher Rebbe[8] explains that the verse is teaching that even before Moshe was born, Miriam, although she was the eldest child, deferred to her brother Aharon and showed him the utmost respect. This had three results. First, Aharon's spiritual qualities grew. Second, Miriam attained the same good qualities that Aharon was noted for: she too became a pursuer of peace. And third, Miriam's latent abilities developed as well.

The Rebbe applied this teaching to the role of a wife. Women excel at kindness. Therefore, they should infuse their actions with an extra dimension of generosity. A woman should express love for her husband even when he is acting far from lovable. Women in particular should strive to cultivate the trait of humility before G-d, emulating our matriarchs Sarah, Rivkah, Rochel, and Leah. The greater a woman's humility, the more she enables her loved ones to flourish and achieve their true potential.

---

[8] See *Likkutei Sichos* vol. 11, pg. 55

POINTS FOR PRACTICAL REFLECTIONS

- Women bear the major responsibility for creating a peaceful home.
- Women are the light in the lives of their loved ones.
- The greater a woman's humility, the more she gains and the more she enables her loved ones to achieve their true potential.
- When a woman puts her husband's will first, he will strive to do her will.
- A wife with a strong faith in G-d gives her husband the ability to focus on serving Him.
- Realistic assessments and expectations of a relationship ensure that the relationship will endure.

The greater a woman's humility, the more she enables her loved ones to flourish and achieve their true potential.

EXERCISES AND MEDITATIONS

Visualize your soul accepting the assignment—willingly and happily—of coming down for the sake of elevating the soul of your husband, in order that you may be reunited again, eternally, in heaven.

Consider the example of women such as Rachel, the wife of Rabbi Akiva, who so readily gave up honor and wealth, and whose devotion was so treasured by her husband.

See yourself as being on that same level, in your devotion to your husband.

(The exercises and meditations of Chapter Six are applicable here as well.)

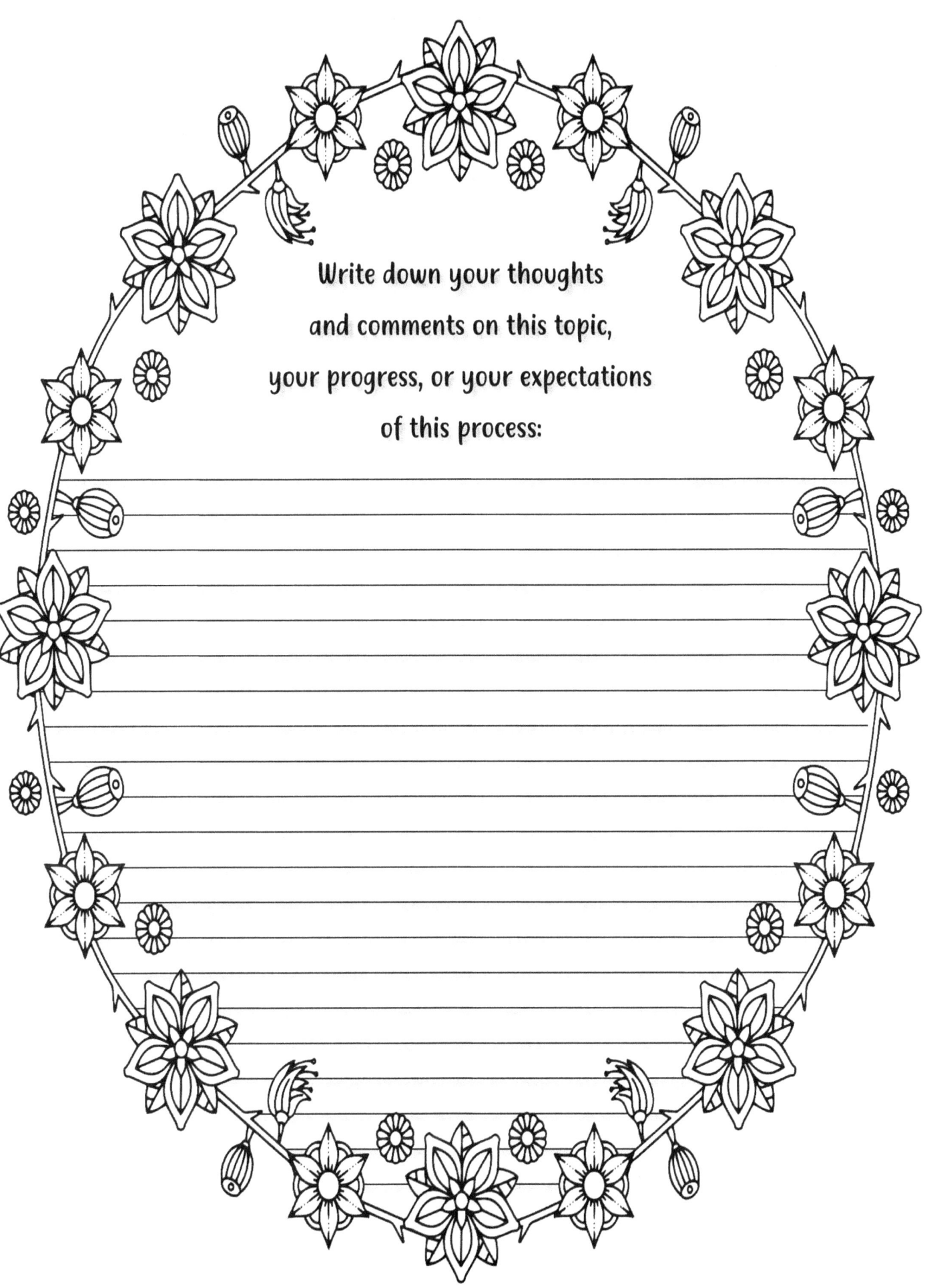

Write down your thoughts and comments on this topic, your progress, or your expectations of this process:

CHAPTER EIGHT
MAN'S ROLE IN MARRIAGE

In the *Tanna D'bei Eliyahu*, Eliyahu (Elijah the Prophet) teaches that "man must be humble in his Torah learning, in his good deeds, and in his fear of Heaven" in all his relationships—as a son, a husband, father, student, and neighbor—"in order that he should be beloved above and pleasant below and accepted by all," because "the Shechinah rests upon whoever is humble."[9]

It is important not to confuse humility with timidity or weakness. It is neither. It is an acceptance of our particular strengths and abilities, along with an understanding of what is expected of us.

Men and women are expected to utilize the particular strengths of their masculine and feminine nature to improve their marriages. Men will approach a problem with a different attitude and from a different perspective than women will, and vice versa. Men naturally tend to self-restraint. A man should therefore discipline himself to restrain his anger and to make a clear demonstration of his love for his wife.

---

[9] Chapter 15, quoted in "*Who's the Man in the House?*"

POINTS FOR PRACTICAL REFLECTIONS

- A husband is obligated to demonstrate care and concern for his wife.
- Your wife came down into this world for your sake.
- A husband should be king in his home but he may not be a tyrant.
- Treat your wife like a queen and she will treat you like a king.
- Honor and respect your wife more than yourself.
- Compliment her by sharing your time, your thoughts, and your daily life with her.
- Do not overly rely on your wife for financial support.
- If your wife is preventing you from doing what you want to do, examine your own actions.
- Correcting yourself will lead to your wife becoming your greatest supporter.

The Shechinah rests upon whoever is humble.

EXERCISES AND MEDITATIONS

Recognize that your wife sacrificed her place in heaven to come down here for your sake.

Visualize her as assisting angel, whose mission is to help you perfect yourself and thereby enable you to reunite with your soulmate in heaven.

Resolve to help her complete her mission. Treat her with the gratitude and appreciation appropriate for such a gracious and loving gesture.

Smile at your wife and greet her pleasantly every morning.

Try to give your wife at least one sincere compliment daily.

Make it a habit to spend a certain amount of time every day, or at least once a week, conversing privately with your wife. If possible, take a walk together. Even a short walk around the block will intensify your feelings of companionship and help you to focus on your status as a couple.

Consider your wife's personality and temperament. Try to imagine what sort of gift or gesture she would appreciate.

Visualize all the steps necessary to procure or produce this wonderful item. Picture yourself presenting it to her; picture her reaction.

Treat your wife like a queen, and she will treat you like a king.

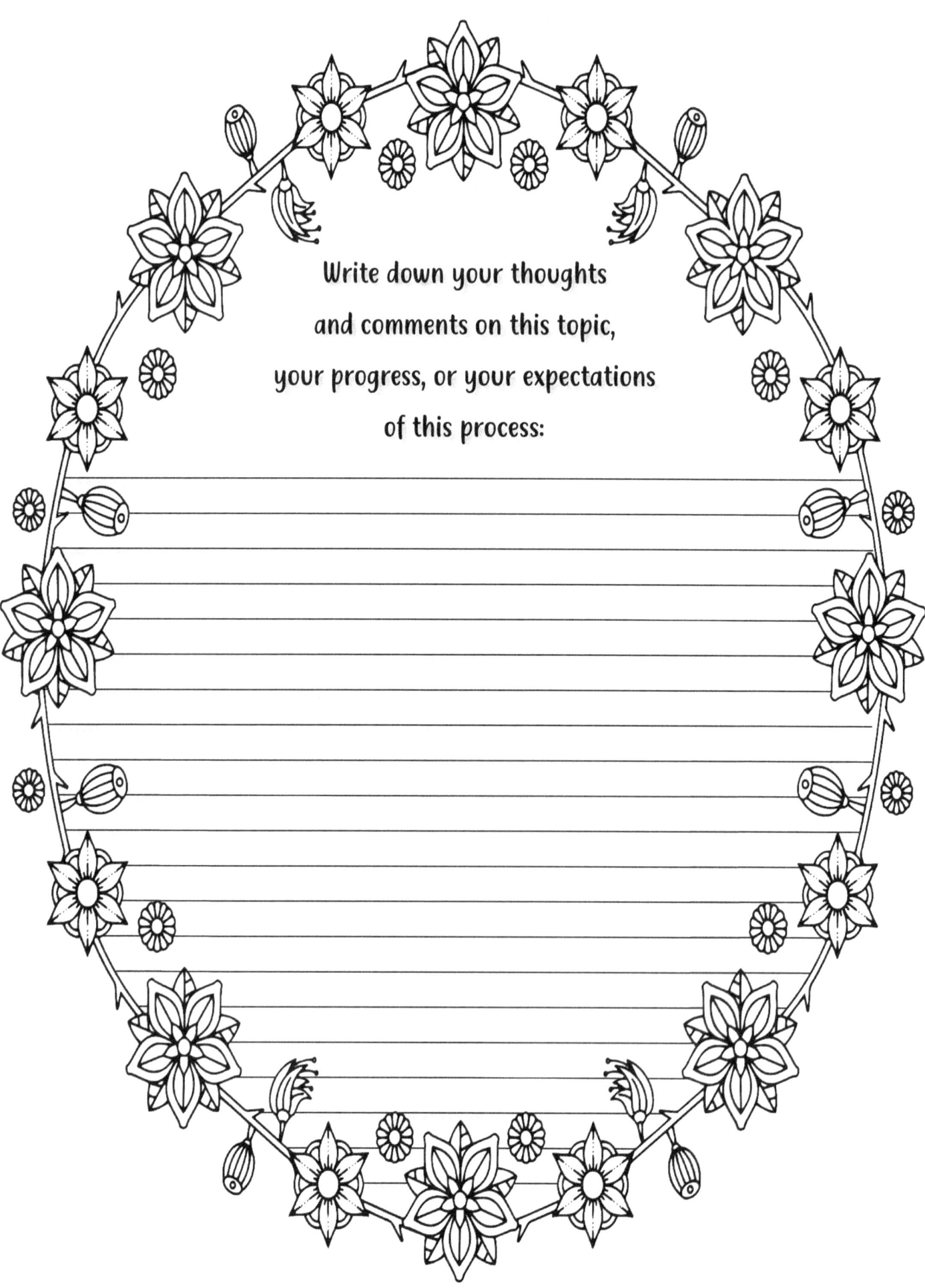

Write down your thoughts and comments on this topic, your progress, or your expectations of this process:

בס"ד

Chapter Nine

CHAPTER NINE
UNITY

When you make the achievement of unity in your home a priority of the highest order, you are empowered by G-d to succeed in this transformation.

You and your spouse have different temperaments and different innate traits. Each one of you, with your own wisdom and abilities, has a unique way of serving Hashem. Nevertheless, the two of you truly form a single unit. Having different roles should not imply any disunity in your relationship.

The Hebrew words for "man" (*ish*) and "woman" (*isha*) each contain the letters *alef* and *shin*, which together spell *aish*, or "fire." This indicates that each spouse has his or her own fire. When they are not worthy, this is a fire of lust, envy, or anger—characteristics that enter a couple's life when the Divine Presence is absent.

The word *ish* contains the letter *yud*, and the word *isha* contains the letter *hey*. When these two letters are combined, they spell one of Hashem's names. This indicates that when the couple refines their characters, that flame becomes a holy fire of love, and G-d dwells in their midst.[10]

Men and women have their own ways of actualizing this holy fire. Do not be discouraged or dismayed if your spouse is not striving for holiness at the same rate that you are, or even attempts to impede your development. Work on fanning your own fire, and eventually your spouse will be warmed by it. The more effort you put into becoming holy, the more G-d will do for you.

---

[10] Ginsburgh, p. 109.

POINTS FOR PRACTICAL REFLECTIONS

- Serve Hashem in your own unique way.
- Encourage your spouse to do so as well.
- Be aware that the efforts of the two of you complement each other.
- Make the achievement of unity in your home a top priority.
- When husband and wife act unselfishly toward each other, they merit that the Shechinah, *aish ocheles aish*, "the fire that consumes all other fires," dwells between them.
- Refining your characters brings a holy fire of love into your lives, and allows G-d to dwell in your midst.
- Challenges can "squeeze out" fine qualities of character within our souls.
- Every couple begins married life with a gift of joy and happiness from G-d.
- With the right attitude and the proper effort, a couple can adorn themselves with more joyous attributes throughout their lives together.

The more effort you put into becoming holy, the more G-d will do for you.

EXERCISES AND MEDITATIONS

Consider two disparate elements which, although very different from each other, unite to form a new and beautiful substance, for example honey and lemon into lemonade.

Visualize the love flowing between the brothers Moshe and Aharon and unifying them, although they were different men with different ways of serving Hashem. Now visualize the love flowing between you and your spouse and unifying the two of you, although you are different human beings with different ways of seeing the world and of serving Hashem.

Think of the ways in which your spouse differs from you, and how that complements you and completes your home. Consider these differences as blessings.

Visualize yourself at home in a very relaxed state. You are aware of the different elements within each individual in your home and you are at peace with them. In this state of serenity, you are able to focus on the virtues of peace in the home. An aura of humility surrounds you, and a yearning for unity within your family that spreads throughout your home. The holiness of your humble thoughts, speech, and actions invite G-d's presence. You feel the warmth of holiness brilliantly radiating throughout your home. There is goodness within all elements of your home. You are happy.

> Work on fanning your own fire, and eventually your spouse will be warmed by it.

Visualize a holy fire within yourself and a holy fire within your spouse. See each of these fires as taking on the shape of a Hebrew letter (*yod* for the husband and *hei* for the wife). Now they join together to form a name of Hashem. Experience yourself and your spouse as two parts of a whole, blended together. Feel that Hashem is dwelling in your midst.

Visualize yourself in a pressurizing, challenging situation. Imagine that as the pressure increases, it is refining and drawing forth your finest qualities, which may have been hidden until now even from your own knowledge. Know that these strengths are now available for you to utilize at any time.

Visualize yourself accepting a large gift-wrapped box. See yourself opening it up with delighted anticipation. Inside you find two beautiful bottles, one marked "joy" and the other "happiness." Imagine that these two bottles are always full and always available for you to pour out some of these feelings and incorporate them into your daily life.

Write down the story of your meeting, courtship, and marriage. Read it as though it were fiction concerning people you don't know. Make note of how G-d directed events for the "characters." Recognize the miracles of your relationship.

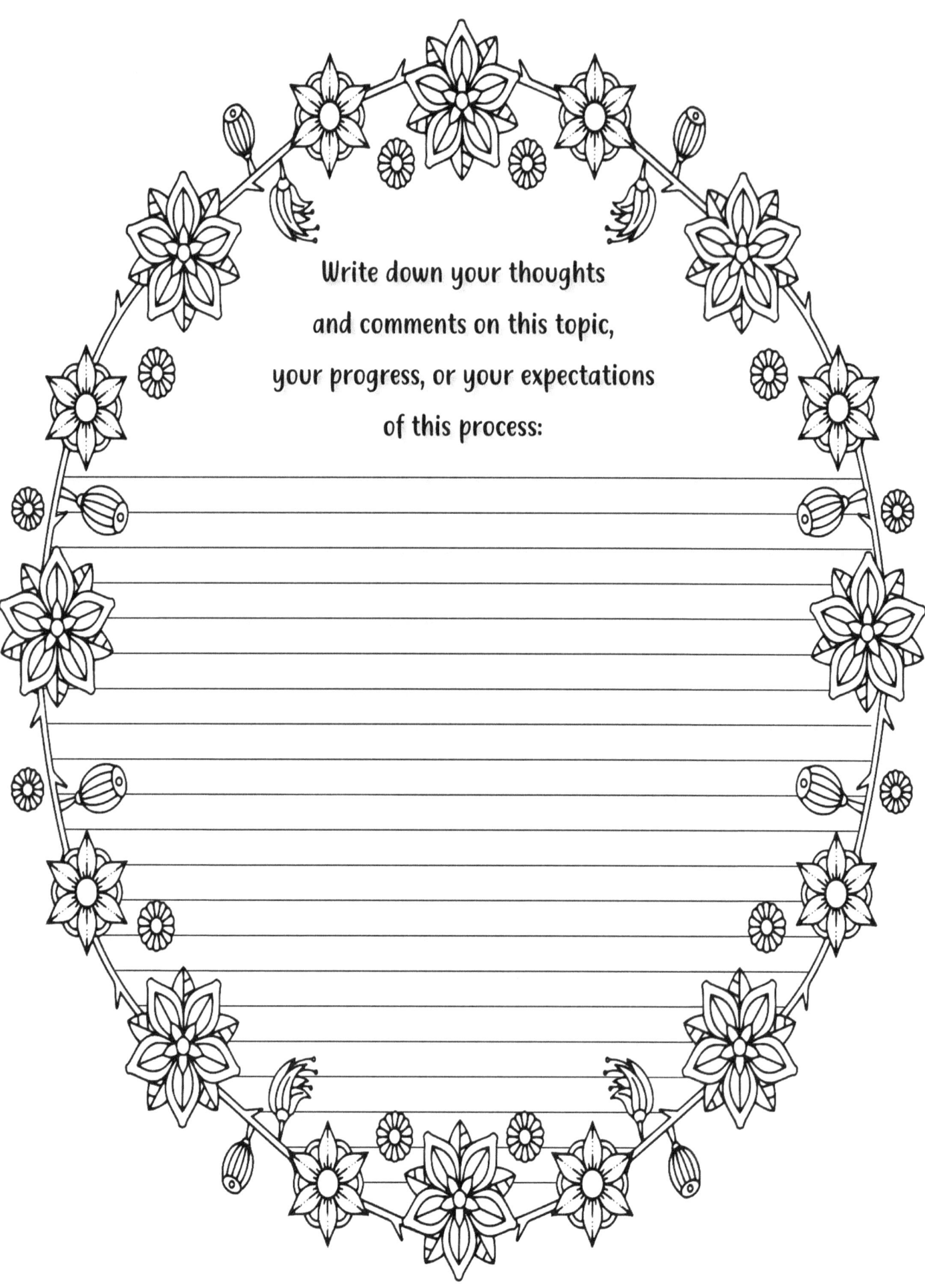

Write down your thoughts and comments on this topic, your progress, or your expectations of this process:

בס"ד

Chapter Ten

CHAPTER TEN
WHY CAN'T WE GET ALONG?

Sometimes two people who are genuine soul mates are actually incompatible. It may be that a soul was destined to endure a difficult marriage as a means of rectification, either of one spouse or of their offspring.[11] As the saying goes, "A smooth sea never made a skillful sailor."

The difficulties in some marriages may arise from deep and invisible roots. We (generally) are not privy to the details of our hidden distant past, but knowing that it may be the possible cause of our present problems can ease our situation and cast it in a more positive light.

Most marital difficulties are of more readily discernible origins. Some extremely common issues are: differing levels of religious observance, maintaining double standards, problems dealing with money, and different expectations and styles of parenting.

These issues may create an uncomfortable atmosphere, but none is an insurmountable obstacle to a good relationship.

---

[11] See *Yevamos* 63b.

POINTS FOR PRACTICAL REFLECTIONS

- An incompatible couple may still be genuine soul mates.
- Marital difficulties may be a rectification for a soul.
- Focus on your position as one of a couple, not an individual: "we" rather than "me."
- Increasing your spirituality can be an effective aid to your relationship.
- Not every soul is on the same level, and certain behaviors may be indicative of the soul's level.
- A "high level" soul requires more maintenance, or more nourishment, to complete its mission here.

As the saying goes, "A smooth sea never made a skillful sailor."

EXERCISES AND MEDITATIONS

When you see a character flaw *in yourself*, say the following affirmations:

"This behavior just shows how holy I really am."

"G-d willing, I will soon channel these holy energies to the good."

When you see a character flaw *in your spouse*, say the following affirmations:

"This behavior just shows how holy my spouse really is."

"G-d willing, he/she will soon channel these holy energies to the good."

Do not react to a difficult marital situation with self-pity; do not focus on feeling disrespected, unloved, dissatisfied, or mistreated. Do not castigate yourself for having made a bad choice in spouses. Instead, change your paradigm from "me" to "we."

Rewrite your internal script along the following lines: "*We* are here to help *each other* gain true respect, love, and honor. Working *together*, *we* can experience joy and happiness, and *our* relationship can be adorned with the other joyous attributes mentioned in the wedding blessing. If *we* haven't yet achieved these goals, *we* are unlikely to advance *our* cause by focusing on what's missing. With determination, hard work, and love, *we* will see positive results."

Actively work on increasing the spirituality in your life and home. A wife may try to ensure that the home is quiet enough for her husband to learn there or that it is sufficiently under control for him to go out to learn. A husband may make it possible for his wife to have more time to *daven* and learn Torah on her own by sharing responsibility for household chores or, if it can be afforded, by hiring someone to help with the housekeeping, or a couple may learn Torah together.

Write down your thoughts and comments on this topic, your progress, or your expectations of this process:

CHAPTER ELEVEN
COMPASSION AND FORGIVENESS

In any relationship, it is imperative to look beyond the surface. You can develop that ability, and recognize the beautiful inner qualities of your spouse. You might ask why you should feel compassionate or forgiving towards your spouse, if he or she is consistently annoying you or causing you pain?

Compassion banishes hatred and increases love. The Zohar teaches us that when you have compassion toward a person who is stuck at a particular point of spiritual and emotional development, those feelings of compassion are the tool that can "redeem" and help release the imprisoned soul. Once liberated, that soul can then love Hashem more freely and act more lovingly toward His creations.

When we have compassion on someone, a feeling of love toward them is aroused within us rather than a feeling of hatred. You may be finding it difficult to feel loving towards your spouse, due to his or her behavior or to some internal struggle of your own. Yet you can overcome this lack of love with compassion. As Rabbi Yaakov Y. Herman famously said, "If you have *rachmanus* (compassion), you don't need *savlanus* (tolerance)." [12]

If the winds of disdain continue to blow through your marriage, ask yourself if you have done your utmost to fulfill the *mitzvah* of loving your fellow as yourself in regard to your spouse. Forgiving your spouse is a vital aspect of maintaining peace in the home. The foundation of forgiveness is empathy for and an understanding of the challenges that your spouse faces.

---

[12] Ruchoma Shain, *All for the Boss*, (New York: Feldheim, 1984) pg. 371

POINTS FOR PRACTICAL REFLECTIONS

- Helping those closest to us is often a great challenge.
- Repay with kindness even someone who has offended you, especially family members.
- Forgiving your spouse is a vital aspect of maintaining peace in the home.
- Painful words may carry a message from Hashem.
- Forgiveness has many benefits.
- Empathy is the foundation of forgiveness.
- Be ready to apologize to your spouse, first and often.
- Praying for the refinement of your own character and that of your spouse is an effective aid in difficult times.

Compassion banishes hatred and increases love.

EXERCISES AND MEDITATIONS

Visualize yourself at the gym. See yourself being drawn to the weights. On the weights are written "compassion." As you lift them, your heart begins to pound and a flow of love begins to pulsate within you. You are stronger now. You are building compassion within yourself.

Consider how old hurts are affecting you now. Do challenges in your current relationships resemble hurts that occurred to you as a child? Acknowledge the pain of yesterday, then let it go.

See yourself walking toward a body of water, carrying two bags. Now you are standing at the water's edge. You open one bag. In this bag are all the hurts from your childhood. You do not need to hold onto that old pain. Affirm out loud, "I choose to let go of my past hurts. I am confident that I can remove my pains of yesterday. I want to have healthy relationships today." Take each negative emotion and throw it into the sea. Watch them all drift away. You feel a sense of release and relief.

Open the second bag and pull out positive emotions such as empathy, compassion, and forgiveness. You are filled with a sense of strength. You feel that you no longer need to protect yourself by withdrawing or growing angry. You feel able to relate to others in a more kind and loving manner.

Visualize yourself standing next to someone who has sinned against you. Focus on that person: see them standing before you, stuck in place, unable to move forward spiritually. Visualize the compassion spilling over from you to that person. See it releasing them to love G-d more freely and fully.

See yourself forgiving that person. Realize that your compassion has released their capacity to love. Your forgiveness has increased their ability to do *teshuvah*.

Sense the change in yourself for the better. Feel your greater dignity and the elevation of your soul.

During the recitation of the *Refa'ainu* prayer, pray to be healed of any past hurts and of any current negativity. Pray also for your spouse, or any person in your life to whom you are having difficulty relating.

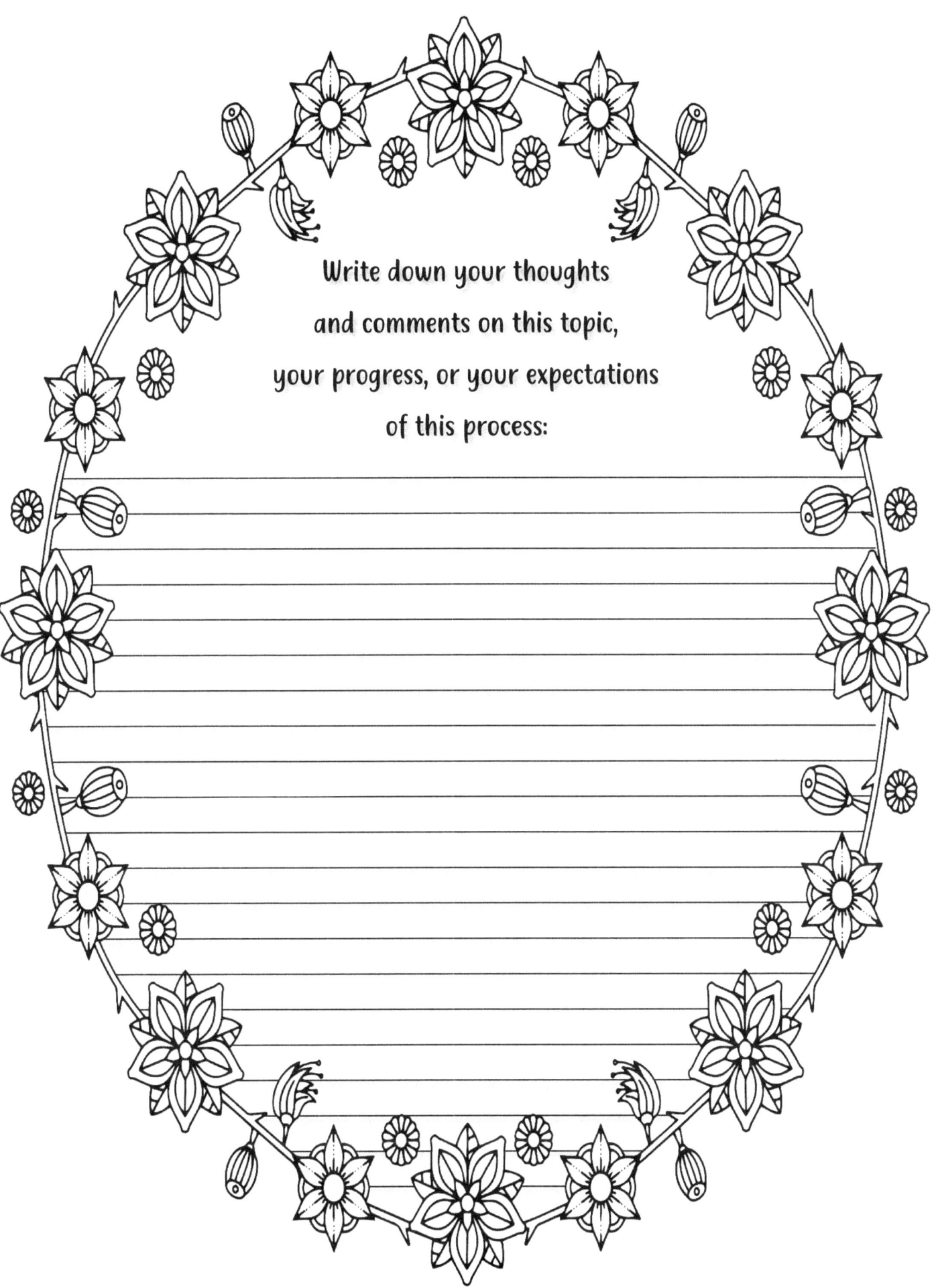

Write down your thoughts and comments on this topic, your progress, or your expectations of this process:

CHAPTER TWELVE
MODEL COMMUNICATION

Perfecting relationships is a lifetime journey, one interaction at a time. The means you use to maintain and enhance the purity of your home should be refined and pleasant. Shlomo Hamelech/King Solomon said of the Torah (Proverbs 3:17), "Her ways are pleasant ways, and all her paths are peace." You are more likely to bring others to a peaceful path if you yourself are walking that path; you are more likely to have a positive influence on your spouse by modeling appropriate behavior yourself.

Positive emotions and actions are will be more successful in helping to increase and maintain holiness in your home and marriage. A major step toward strengthening the bonds between you and your spouse is to upgrade your level of communication with your partner, to be more emotionally open and affectionate, even when your expectations are not being met. When you act more lovingly, that induces your spouse to respond in kind.

During contentious moments, engage in some positive thinking to help regain your inner strength and outer calm. Remember that provocations with your partner are meant to help you become more patient, understanding, and tolerant.

If you have had a conflict with your spouse, do not confront him or her while you are still angry. Wait until your anger dissipates and the atmosphere is calm before initiating a discussion. Limit this talk to your most essential concerns.

Before beginning this conversation, envision yourself using empathetic, compassionate, and healing words that you would like to hear your spouse use when talking to you.

Start the conversation with words of appreciation to your spouse for sharing time with you.

While you are speaking, pay attention to body signals: if you feel your stomach in knots, your nose flaring, your face growing hot, or your voice rising, then take a deep breath or two until you calm down.

When you are finished, verbalize your feeling of resolution.

End the conversation with another expression of appreciation, to reaffirm your bond.

Remember that provocations with your partner are meant to help you become more patient, understanding, and tolerant.

POINTS FOR PRACTICAL REFLECTIONS

- Model the behavior you wish to see in others.
- Pleasant ways will accomplish more than force.
- Improved communication leads to improved relationships.
- Do not respond in the heat of the moment.
- Address contentious issues when you are calm and prepared.
- Avoid overwhelming yourself or your spouse: prioritize and limit the number of issues to be addressed.
- Preface your discussion with words of appreciation for your spouse.
- End the discussion by expressing appreciation to your spouse for cooperating and sharing time with you.

When you act more lovingly, that induces your spouse to respond in kind.

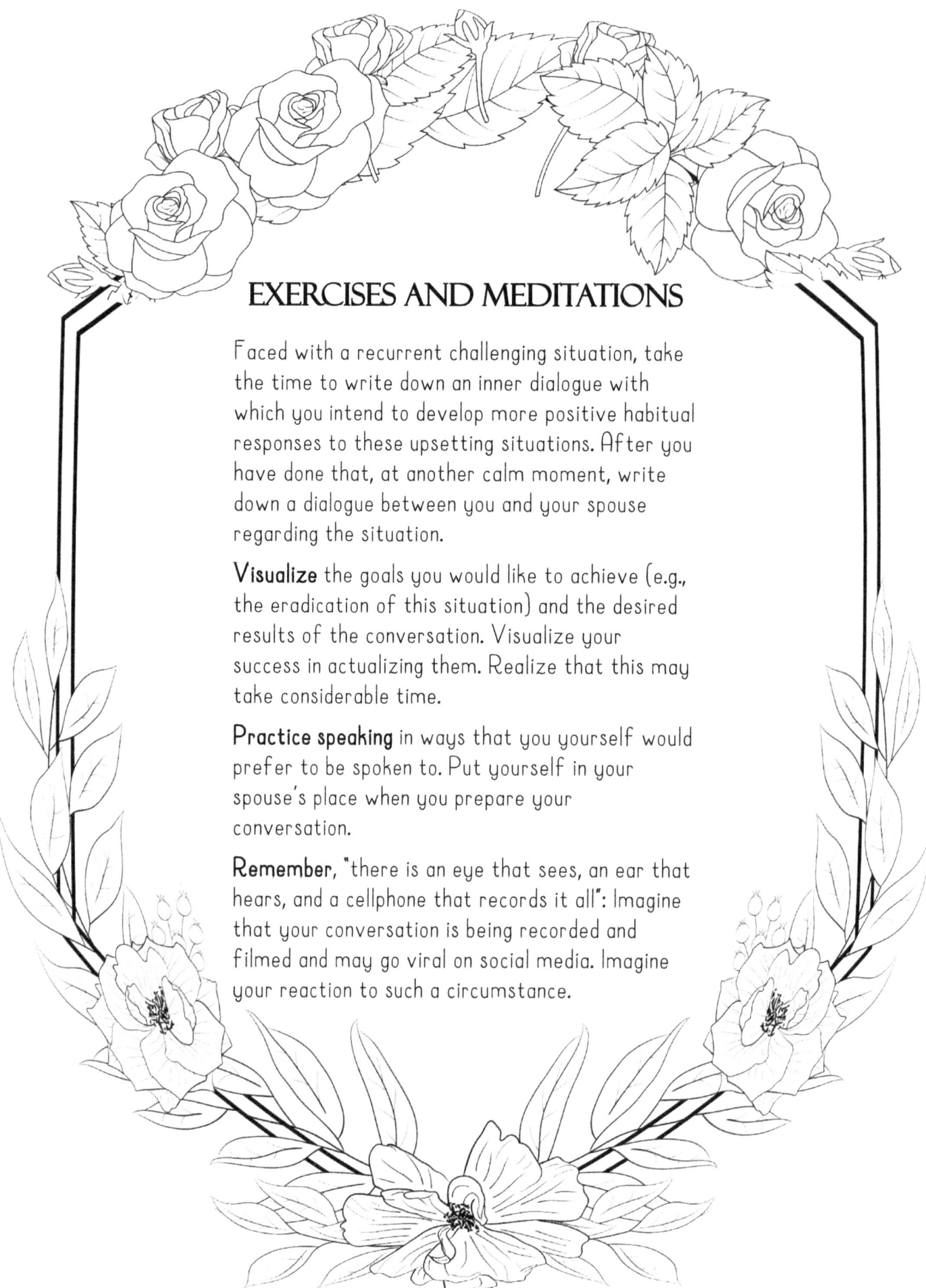

EXERCISES AND MEDITATIONS

Faced with a recurrent challenging situation, take the time to write down an inner dialogue with which you intend to develop more positive habitual responses to these upsetting situations. After you have done that, at another calm moment, write down a dialogue between you and your spouse regarding the situation.

Visualize the goals you would like to achieve (e.g., the eradication of this situation) and the desired results of the conversation. Visualize your success in actualizing them. Realize that this may take considerable time.

Practice speaking in ways that you yourself would prefer to be spoken to. Put yourself in your spouse's place when you prepare your conversation.

Remember, "there is an eye that sees, an ear that hears, and a cellphone that records it all": Imagine that your conversation is being recorded and filmed and may go viral on social media. Imagine your reaction to such a circumstance.

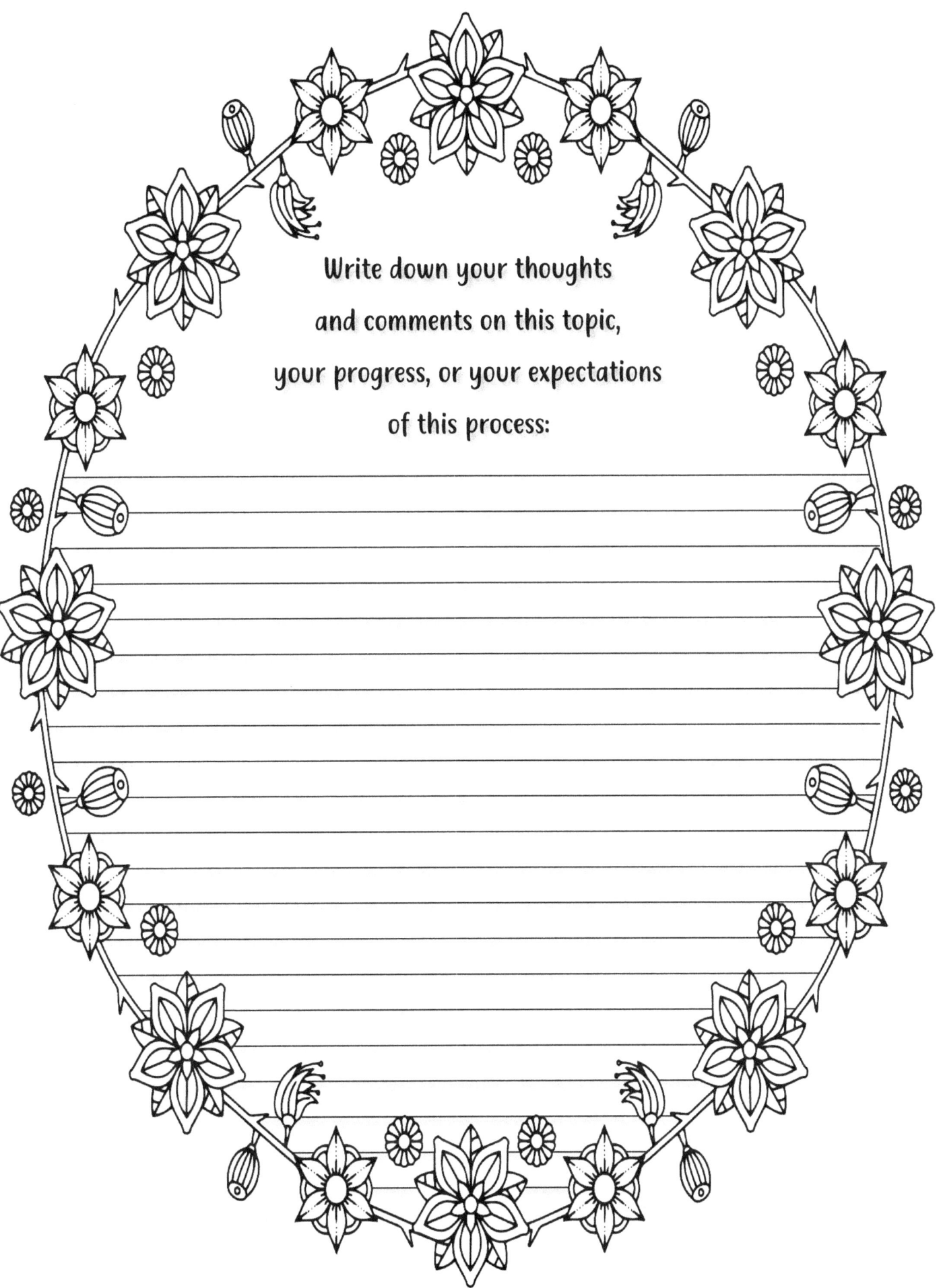

Write down your thoughts and comments on this topic, your progress, or your expectations of this process:

בס"ד

CHAPTER THIRTEEN
SHALOM BAYIS AND PARENTING

The topic of child-rearing deserves a book of its own. However, it should be discussed here in brief with an emphasis on its connection to *shalom bayis*.

The Torah teaches us that no element of life is devoid of meaning and purpose, and that every interaction is divinely designed. Relationships are an important process that leads to completion (*shleimus*). Our relationships have real and measurable consequences on our lives and those around us. The quality of our closest relationships profoundly affects how we feel about ourselves. The way we communicate both verbally and non-verbally affects the emotional, cognitive, and physical development of our children, as well as our own physical and mental health.

Child-rearing is complex. Each child is a unique, dynamic individual who changes almost daily. For parents to properly guide their children, it is important to consider the environment that the parents create at home.

Rebbetzin Chanie Geisinsky, my *mashpia* (mentor) describes successful child-rearing as 50% consistent *chinuch* (Jewish education) and 50% *shalom bayis*. A healthy relationship between you and your spouse is critical to the success of every aspect of your child's healthy development, both physical and spiritual. Treating your spouse positively in front of your children is paramount. When husband and wife get along and demonstrate respect for each other, it helps the children get along better, and also lays a foundation for children to respect their parents.

POINTS FOR PRACTICAL REFLECTIONS

- Your family members are the most precious part of your life.
- Raising your voice in anger, speaking sarcastically, or otherwise belittling your spouse or children is very damaging to *shalom bayis* and to the emotional health of your family.
- A parent must model the qualities of thoughtfulness, sensitivity, and generosity that will set the standards for the children.
- Consider that if your children treat you disrespectfully, you may have done something to warrant that.
- Children experience many difficult moments throughout their day; make your home a place of happy moments for them.
- Professional counseling that is sensitive to Torah ethics and values may be useful in helping you achieve healthier perspectives on your marriage.

A healthy relationship between you and your spouse is critical to the success of every aspect of your child's healthy development.

EXERCISES AND MEDITATIONS

Picture yourself remaining calm in front of your family even when you feel like indulging in an emotional outburst. Concentrate on how precious your family is to you, until you can control the impulse to act unkindly towards them.

Repeat the following affirmations throughout the day, even before a challenging situation arises:

"I want to unite, not to win."

"I want peace, not victory."

"Making peace is the greatest victory."

"My goal is to give peace of mind, not *pieces* of my mind."

"*Shalom bayis* is the surest path to raising emotionally healthy children."

"My efforts to become a positive role model will maximize my success as a parent."

Plan to avoid fighting in front of the child(ren). If you think you might give in to your urge to fight, turn around and walk away.

Recognize that when you don't walk away, you are putting your need to vent ahead of your children's well-being and peace of mind.

After you walk away, write down all your thoughts and feelings on the situation, so you can discuss it later when the children aren't around.

Have your discussion somewhere private, with minimal distractions and interruptions. Deal with your spouse closely and personally. Express your needs to your partner calmly and clearly. Be specific; he or she may not know what those needs are.

Work out the problem with cooperation, not competition.

Write down your thoughts and comments on this topic, your progress, or your expectations of this process:

CHAPTER FOURTEEN
GRATITUDE AND PATIENCE

No matter what you are going through, no matter what mood you may find yourself in, recognize that all events are orchestrated by Hashem, Who is compassionate and Who alone knows what is best for you. It is for us to thank and praise G-d for all that He does for us, whether or not we can clearly understand how it is for our benefit.

My goal has been to help you build a harmonious and joyful relationship with your spouse. The best way to do that is to strengthen your relationship with G-d, through a growing appreciation of His love for you and His plan for you. That strength will help you motivate yourself to work on refining your character, which in turn will lead you to achieve a fulfilling marriage.

Now that you are coming to the end of this book, give it to your spouse to read. Review it regularly by yourself, and perhaps, occasionally with your spouse. My hope is that you will take its messages to heart until they become a part of you. If you feel that you need further assistance, I am always available to help you with individualized counseling.

If you find that you are not seeing the results that you seek in your relationship, don't lose hope. To those who were on the verge of giving up on their efforts, the Lubavitcher Rebbe provided the example of the date palm: although it takes up to 70 years to mature, its dates are among the sweetest of all fruits.

My blessing to you, dear reader, is that you too will taste the sweetness of a healthy, happy, mature marriage. Remember, every kind act beautifies us. Every kind act to our spouse also completes us. Every step across the bridge of kindness brings us closer to our spouse, closer to Moshiach, and closer to G-d.

POINTS FOR PRACTICAL REFLECTIONS

- Remember G-d is orchestrating your life.
- Try to maintain a healthy perspective.
- Perspective makes it easy to cultivate an attitude of gratitude.
- Gratitude leads to a feeling of security.
- Emotional security brings peace and harmony to a home.
- Reviewing your actions daily leads to repentance, repentance leads to humility, humility leads to harmony.
- To strengthen your relationship with your spouse, strengthen your relationship with G-d.
- Achieving good things takes time.
- Every kind deed is another step on the bridge of kindness.

All events are orchestrated by Hashem, Who is compassionate and Who alone knows what is best for you.

EXERCISES AND MEDITATIONS

When you say *Modeh Ani* ("I thank You") in the morning, think of all the good in your life for which you can feel grateful to G-d: the parts of your body that are healthy and functioning; a roof over your head; the people you share your life with; your abilities and talents and the opportunities to use them.

At a quiet time of the day, sit down and make a detailed list of other items that you can add to your *Modeh Ani* meditation.

Note the areas in your marital relationship in which you think you still need to improve.

Pick one aspect to work on for three weeks (bearing in mind that a habit takes at least that long to break). If, for example, you resolve to maintain a pleasant tone of voice when communicating with your spouse, practice speaking in that tone when you are alone. Write out possible responses to comments by your spouse on topics you think are likely to arise.

Reward yourself for having come this far, and for every additional step you take.

Reward your spouse, too.

Every step across the bridge of kindness brings us closer to our spouse, closer to Moshiach, and closer to G-d.

Write down your thoughts and comments on this topic, your progress, or your expectations of this process:

ACKNOWLEDGMENTS

This book, like all the other volumes in the *Reaching New Heights* series, is the effort of a team of professional, skilled, and talented individuals. My deepest gratitude goes to Ella Matayeva, whose idea it was to distill the information in my book into a hands-on, interactive workbook, and Rae Shagalov, whose creative artistry brought it to beautiful life. Special thanks to Reva S. Baer for her comprehensive editorial services.

I must acknowledge Dr. John Biroc of CSU Northridge, who many years ago introduced me to the world of meditation and inspired me to delve into its possibilities, and Dr. Levy of Pepperdine University, who gave me the opportunity to co-direct programs for the psychodrama and meditation groups at the Halfway House Mental Health Center in Santa Monica. Both went beyond the call of duty in my training and supervision.

I would like to thank two special colleagues and dear friends: Chana Kaiman, who gave me many opportunities to present therapist training workshops in international conferences and to co-author articles on a variety of mental health issues, and Esther Kenigsberg of SPARKS, the support organization for Pre-and Post-Natal difficulties, who has provided me with continuous training in the field of mental health.

DEDICATIONS

To my dear parents Esther Levy and Gabriel Levy, gratitude for their *mesiras nefesh* (self-sacrifice) to ensure I had a Jewish education and for always being there for me.

To my dear real soul sisters, Ruth Himmelman and Chana Levy, and their families.

To my children Yechezkal Moshe and Menucha Rochel, and Chana Leah, thank you for being you. Thank you for your love and friendship and for being my wonderful partners, the ultimate catalysts for my personal development. Since you were born, not a day has gone by without a prayer in my heart that I could be, for you, the best mother and a shining example of a true Jew. Your presence in my life has motivated me to search for the deepest truths. My yearning to share these treasures with you—and with others—is captured and made manifest in all my work.

To my dear husband, the other half of my soul, David Yerushalmi—to paraphrase Rabbi Akiva, "Everything that is mine, is his." He has always believed in me and always supported me in all my projects, in every way. May Hashem bless him in every way.

To my dear Lubavitcher Rebbe, Rabbi Menachem Mendel Schneerson, and all our Rebbes, for all the *mesiras nefesh* of their lives and their life's work.

Ultimately, I owe my thanks to Hashem for His care and His kindness, for leading me to Torah and opening my heart to the inner dimensions of Chassidus.

May Hashem bless each and every one of you and your families forever!!!

Dedicated with gratitude and admiration to
Rabbi Dr. Abraham J. Twerski, z"l
הרב אברהם יהושע העשיל בן הרב יעקב ישראל ז"ל

And
Rabbi Aharon Yaakov ben Harav Mordechai Eliyohu Schwei z"l
הרב אהרן יעקב בן הרב מרדכי אליהו שוויי ז"ל

Who gave of themselves endlessly, tirelessly,
and with great self-sacrifice
on behalf of our people,
and whom I was privileged
to learn from and work with.
Forever grateful for their time,
their expertise, and their caring.

In loving memory of
Bezalel Jacobson
and
Shlomo Jacobson

And
In honor of
Their loving wife
and mother
Faigie Jacobson
A one-woman chessed powerhouse
Who keeps open
her home
and her heart
For those in need

In loving memory of
Ron Itzhak ben Zelik and Zelik Ben Leon Lev
May their neshamot be elevated and
their memories be for a blessing.

In honor of the first wedding anniversary
of my son and daughter-in-law
Yechezkal Moshe and Menucha Rochel

With deepest appreciation to the sponsors
of this publication:

Shneor Zalmon and Yehudis Hickson
and family

Jason Zaiderman and family

Devorah Hakimian

ABOUT MIRIAM YERUSHALMI

With an MS in Psychology and Marriage and Family Counseling from Pepperdine University (1990), Miriam works in private practice with families and children, and, through her organization SANE, volunteers many hours providing a resource for the neediest to access appropriate Mental Health care.

Uniquely skilled at combining behavioral and humanistic approaches to address a wide spectrum of psychopathology, including ADHD, addiction, anxiety, depressive disorders, panic disorders, and anger management, Miriam imparts self-regulation brain training techniques whereby clients learn to develop tools for a balanced and fulfilled life.

Miriam's approach, CBTT™, fuses fundamental Torah principles with her background in Mental Health to empower individuals to release their inner healing potential, while aligning with their true purpose on essential life issues.

A sought-after speaker, Miriam lectures internationally. She has hundreds of classes available, for adults and children, on TorahAnytime.com, TorahCafé.com, the SPARKS helpline, and her own websites. She writes regularly for publications including *The Jewish Press, Chabad.org, True Balance,* and *Table for Five,* and has presented workshops at the annual Nefesh conference for therapists. As a counselor for SPARKS, Miriam gives teleconferences and webinars on many topics relevant to emotional and spiritual development. Miriam has also taught weekly classes in the central synagogue in Crown Heights, NY (770) as well as in Long Island, for over 20 years.

CHILDREN'S BOOKS BY MIRIAM YERUSHALMI

Available on Amazon.com

Also available in Hebrew & Yiddish

Also available in Hebrew & Yiddish

Also available in Hebrew & Yiddish

Also available in Yiddish

Also available in Yiddish

Also available in Yiddish

Also available in Yiddish

Also available in Yiddish

Also available in Yiddish

Also available in Yiddish

Also available in Spanish

ADULT BOOKS BY MIRIAM YERUSHALMI

Available on Amazon.com

COMING SOON:

Chaim Becomes a True Prince

Yossi's New Normal

Brain Train

Bais Hamikdash Within

Reaching New Heights Through Healthier Cooking

Reaching New Heights Through Living Tanya

BOOK MIRIAM YERUSHALMI FOR YOUR NEXT ONLINE OR IN-PERSON RETREAT OR WORKSHOP!

At these retreats, Miriam teaches you to successfully:

- Develop real compassion
- Experience compassion as a cure for the challenges of our times
- Tolerate the negative traits of those you love
- Remember to look into your own "garden"
- Understand what it means to be truly giving
- Unleash the power of forgiveness
- Use positive thoughts and behavior to put out the "fire" of anger
- Master Positive Parenting
- Develop peace in the home
- Communicate your disagreements calmly

PLUS

- Special tips for Men/Fathers
- Special tips for Women/Mothers

Contact Miriam to book an online or in-person retreat or workshop:
www.saveaneshamausa.org
www.reachingnewheightsmy.com

ABOUT RAE SHAGALOV

Rae Shagalov is a Jewish book designer, master calligrapher, and creativity coach who has been developing and refining her craft for over 30 years. She is famous for her beautiful handwriting, which can be viewed, along with more of her artwork and books, at www.holysparks.com.

Rae is the author/illustrator of many books, including *The Secret Art of Talking to G-d*, *Create Your Joyfully Jewish Life*, and *The Joyfully Jewish Family & Adult Coloring Book*.

Rae also helps creative Jewish women and children accomplish their goals and launch their fabulous ideas into the world. In Rae's Passion Projects Mastermind program, she'll show you how to use your 11 kabbalistic Soul Powers (according to Chassidus) to balance your life and/or business, get your creative juices flowing, and get the support and accountability you need to get your special project out into the world!

Perhaps you have an idea or project that tugs at your heart and soul and says, "DO ME!" Or you have a passion project (or a dozen of them) and feel stuck, and don't know where to start. Or maybe you have a great idea, but you're spending way too much time procrastinating and not making much progress. Join other Jewish influencers, moms, bubbies, and fascinating women in Rae's Passion Project Mastermind groups.

FIND OUT MORE AT:
WWW.CREATIVEJEWISHSOUL.COM
WWW.HOLYSPARKS.COM

www.ingramcontent.com/pod-product-compliance
Lightning Source LLC
Chambersburg PA
CBHW081112080526
44587CB00021B/3563